CONSTELLATIONS

Like the future itself, the imaginative possibilities of science fiction are limitless. And the very development of cinema is inextricably linked to the genre, which, from the earliest depictions of space travel and the robots of silent cinema to the immersive 3D wonders of contemporary blockbusters, has continually pushed at the boundaries. **Constellations** provides a unique opportunity for writers to share their passion for science fiction cinema in a book-length format, each title devoted to a significant film from the genre. Writers place their chosen film in a variety of contexts – generic, institutional, social, historical – enabling **Constellations** to map the terrain of science fiction cinema from the past to the present... and the future.

'This stunning, sharp series of books fills a real need for authoritative, compact studies of key science fiction films. Written in a direct and accessible style by some of the top critics in the field, brilliantly designed, lavishly illustrated and set in a very modern typeface that really shows off the text to best advantage, the volumes in the **Constellations** series promise to set the standard for SF film studies in the 21st century.'
Wheeler Winston Dixon, Ryan Professor of Film Studies, University of Nebraska

 Constellations

 Constelbooks

Also available in this series

12 Monkeys Susanne Kord

Blade Runner Sean Redmond

Brainstorm Joseph Maddrey

Children of Men Dan Dinello

Close Encounters of the Third Kind Jon Towlson

The Damned Nick Riddle

Dune Christian McCrea

Ex Machina Joshua Grimm

Inception David Carter

Jurassic Park Paul Bullock

Lost Brigid Cherry

Mad Max Martyn Conterio

RoboCop Omar Ahmed

Rollerball Andrew Nette

Stalker Jon Hoel

Forthcoming

Aliens Cristina Massaccesi

Minority Report D. Harlan Wilson

Moon Brian J Robb

Mr Freedom Tyler Sage

CONSTELLATIONS

The Stepford Wives

Samantha Lindop

Acknowledgements

Foremost, I want to acknowledge my colleague and mentor Professor Tom O'Regan who sadly passed away shortly before the completion of this book. Tom's enthusiasm and praise for this project and for my work more broadly was consistently generous and greatly valued. He will be fondly remembered and deeply missed. I also extend my sincerest gratitude to Constellations series editor John Atkinson for his professionalism and support throughout the process, despite the craziness of COVID-19 and post-truth politics. Further, a special thank you to my anonymous reviewer for their invaluable feedback and overwhelmingly positive evaluation of this research on *The Stepford Wives* universe and its place in the histories of fictional imaginings about artificial women.

First published in 2022 by
Auteur, an imprint of
Liverpool University Press,
4 Cambridge Street,
Liverpool L69 7ZU
www.liverpooluniversitypress.co.uk/imprints/Auteur/
Copyright © Auteur 2022

Series design: Nikki Hamlett at Cassels Design
Set by Cassels Design, Luton, UK.

All rights reserved. No part of this publication may be reproduced in any material form (including photocopying or storing in any medium by electronic means and whether or not transiently or incidentally to some other use of this publication) without the permission of the copyright owner.

Figures from *The Stepford Wives* are © Palomar Pictures International/Fadsin Cinema Associates.

British Library Cataloguing-in-Publication Data
A catalogue record for this book is available from the British Library

ISBN paperback: 978-1-80085-937-1
ISBN hardback: 978-1-80085-936-4
ISBN ePub: 978-1-80085-813-8
ISBN PDF: 978-1-80085-853-4

Contents

Introduction 7

Chapter 1: *The Stepford Wives*, Levin and the Gothic 15
    The Uncanny and the Gothic 15
    The Female Gothic 19
    Rosemary's Baby and the Gothic 21
    The Urban Gothic 24
    The Suburban Gothic 26

Chapter 2: Automatons, Androids, and Stepford Wives 33
    Early Automations 34
    Science, Electricity, and Rationality 37
    Galvanic Miracles and Machine Women 41
    Sci-Fi Cinema and Fembots 47

Chapter 3: *Stepford Wives* in Hollywood 53
    The US Film Industry in the '70s 53
    Making *The Stepford Wives* 56

Chapter 4: *The Stepford Wives* and Liberal Feminism 65
    Feminist Diatribe or 'Rip Off'? 66
    Limits of *The Feminine Mystique* 72
    She's Crazy, Just Crazy 76
    Stepford and the Torment of Sisyphus 81

Chapter 5: *Stepford* Sequels 85
    Happy Pills and Payback 85
    Stepford Husbands and Backlash 89
    Stepford Children, Patriarchal Rage, and Alien Invasion 92

Chapter 6: *The Stepford* Remake – from Sci-Fi Thriller to Farce?................................... 99

    Postfeminist Popular Culture and Oz's Stepford... 102

    Postfeminism and Techno-Anxiety in *Stepford II* 105

Chapter 7: Stepford Wives in the Real World... 109

    Sex Dolls and Sex Robots.. 110

    Heterotopias, Ubiquitous Computing, and the Posthuman 116

    Female Androids on Screen in an Age of Deep Machine Learning....................... 120

Concluding Comments 127

References.. 131

End Notes 141

Introduction

It is rare that a fictional title becomes lexicon, but Ira Levin's 1972 novel *The Stepford Wives*, and the soon-to-follow film adaptation by Bryan Forbes in 1975, is an exception. The phrase 'Stepford wife' has sustained cultural currency as a signifier for a particular kind of middle-class woman who is bound to a patriarchal definition of femininity: a wife who has no life and 'is almost literally an automaton' (Williams 2007, p.85). Indeed, one need not have read the book, nor seen the film, to be familiar with the concept. *The Stepford Wives* has inspired films such as *Disturbing Behaviour* (David Nutter, 1998) and more recently *Get Out* (Jordan Peele, 2017). There have been several made-for-television sequels, including *The Revenge of the Stepford Wives* (Robert Fuest, 1980), *The Stepford Children* (Alan J. Levi, 1987), and *The Stepford Husbands* (Fred Walton, 1996), as well as Investigation Discovery channel's *Secret Lives of Stepford Wives* (2014). There is also Frank Oz's 2004 reimagining of the film starring a high-profile cast including Bette Midler, Glenn Close, Nicole Kidman, Matthew Broderick, and Christopher Walken.

Like many cult films, *The Stepford Wives* did not do especially well at the box office after its initial North American release and critical responses were polarising. Though intended as a feminist diatribe, *The Stepford Wives* was read by many at the time as anti-feminist. Even prominent women's rights activist Betty Friedan, whose 1963 book *The Feminist Mystique* is literalised in the film, was reportedly outraged, declaring it a 'rip-off of the feminist movement' (Klemesrud, 1975, p.29). Other censures levelled at *The Stepford Wives* suggest it may have touched some raw nerves with its unapologetic anti-male sentiment and its dystopic visions of suburban, middle-class America and the nuclear family. On the contrary, the film has been acclaimed for its articulation of some of the most salient ideological and political concerns of liberal feminist activism at the time, including the gender politics of housework and the mindless veneration of cleanliness. This, along with its scathing critique of patriarchal attitudes towards women and their bodies, explored from the female protagonist's subjective position, has contributed to the film's cult status today, as well as attributing to its standing as an important socio-cultural document in its own right.

Furthermore, *The Stepford Wives* has far broader cultural resonance. The film foreshadows what was later to become known as a 'backlash' against feminism – a term conceived by journalist Susan Faludi in 1991 to describe rhetoric that began circulating in mainstream media in the 1980s that feminism was a failed experiment. Backlash theory forms the foundation of more complex ideas about the role of postfeminist discourses and ideologies, including the way they operate to restabilise gender power structures that have been disrupted by the political, economic, and legislative gains of earlier feminist movements. Postfeminism is complex and contradictory, but some of its more salient features involve an ambivalent, depoliticised attitude towards feminism, including the idea that feminism has been achieved and is no longer necessary. Postfeminism celebrates some aspects of feminism – mainly those that have to do with consumerism and choice, but at the same time retrograde ideas about traditional gender roles are equally romanticised and endorsed, including those to do with the mystique of femininity (see McRobbie, 2009, pp.11-12; Negra, 2009, pp.4-5; Tasker and Negra, 2007, p.4).

Not only does *The Stepford Wives* warn of a push-back against feminism, the replacement of real women with mechanical duplicates is foretelling of real world development in social robotics and artificial intelligence (AI). In contrast to industrial and military robots, social robots are intended to be comprehensively integrated into everyday life. It is anticipated that they will become increasingly useful for a variety of interpersonal tasks, particularly those related to domestic help and companionship. While social robots come in many forms, the kinds of machines that receive the most media attention are those designed to look like hyper-feminised women. There is also a growing market for state-of-the-art sex dolls with integrated AI technologies. Far from being a novelty, it is anticipated that as social and sex robots become progressively sophisticated, so too will it become increasingly commonplace for humans to develop deep emotional and sexual attachments to their automated companions (Levy, 2009, p.22). In recent film and television, female robots are likewise experiencing resurgence in popularity. Many of these screen texts destabilise long held imaginings about female robots as subservient to the men who created them. Instead, the machine women enact revenge on the humans who use and abuse them. Alex Garland's sci-fi thriller *Ex Machina* (2015), the television show

Westworld (HBO, 2016–) and AMC's series *Humans* (2015–2018), based on the Swedish series *Äkta Människor* (*Real Humans*, 2012–2014) are just some examples. This suggests that robot women are not static figures, rather they are a product of the socio-cultural and socio-political climate of their creation.

This book takes a longitudinal approach in analysing the *The Stepford Wives* and the larger *Stepford* universe. Fantasies about creating artificial women date back to antiquity with tales like Ovid's *Pygmalion* and later, following industrialisation, stories such as E.T.A Hoffmann's *Der Sandmann* (1816) and Auguste Villiers de l'Isle- Adams' *L'Eve Future* (1886).[1] These historical perspectives give weight to *The Stepford Wives* as a pivotal text that mobilises age-old imaginings about replica women as a plot device and as allegory for some of the more pressing concerns of liberal feminist activism of the 1960s and 1970s. Following a brief synopsis of the film, the book will begin by examining *The Stepford Wives* in the framework of the gothic – a style that permeates the film visually, thematically, and narratively. Originating in eighteenth-century literature, the gothic explores subjects of isolation, entrapment, unsettling places, and treacherous people who are not what they seem. Female-centred gothic further focuses on the psychological and social experiences of women, particularly in relation to their disempowerment in patriarchal power structures. The gothic is central to Levin's work, which the film follows closely in its adaption. This first chapter focuses primarily on Levin's novels, particularly the hugely successful *Rosemary's Baby* (1967) and Levin's use of gothic themes and motifs with the aim of providing a deeper, more inclusive context to the literary pedigree from which *The Stepford Wives* derives. Additionally, this chapter will explore the significance of the suburban gothic; a sub-set of the style that has to do with feelings of disenfranchisement generated by the uncanny liminal spaces of the 'burbs.

Chapter 2 situates *The Stepford Wives* in relation to historical imaginings about artificial women. Of particular focus are fictions from the 1800s – a period of scientific rationality when critical debates about the nature of life, initiated by experiments in galvanic resurrection, pioneered by Italian physician Luigi Galvani in the late 1700s were capturing the popular imagination. It is around this time that gothic science fiction emerged as a sub-genre that amalgamates themes of scientific experimentation with established traditions of classic gothic fiction: a fusion made famous by Mary Shelley's *Frankenstein: Or, the Modern Prometheus* (1823). The idea of galvanic revitalisation coupled with Cartesian logic that life could be separate from the physical arrangement of the body, proved a seductive formula for nineteenth-century physicians and authors alike. A foremost fiction that indulges these ideas – and one especially important to *The Stepford Wives* – is *L'Eve Future*. This chapter will establish the relevance of *L'Eve Future* as an exemplary forerunner to *The Stepford Wives*, as well as to depictions of artificial women in sci-fi cinema more broadly.

Focus will then shift to the making of *The Stepford Wives* in Chapter 3. In particular, the discussion will concentrate on the Hollywood film industry in the 1970s and the various frictions taking place on set during the production of *The Stepford Wives*, especially between Forbes and William Goldman, who authored the screenplay. This chapter will touch on audience responses to the film. However, critical feminist reactions, as well as the film's allegiance to the political imperatives of Friedan's *Feminine Mystique* and liberal feminism more broadly will be explored in-depth in Chapter 4. Friedan describes 'the feminine mystique' as a regressive patriarchal myth about femininity that women were indoctrinated to aspire to following World War II. According to Friedan, this created a silent crisis for (white, middle-class) housewives: trying to live up to the mystique of femininity was leaving them feeling desperate, empty, and neurotic. Friedan terms these unspoken sensations as 'the problem that has no name' (1963, p.19). This chapter examines how *The Stepford Wives* creatively engages with key issues to do with housewifery raised by Friedan and other activists at the time. The chapter will also offer an important critical analysis of Friedan's work in light of subsequent scholarship by prominent theorists such as bell hooks.

The purpose of this book is to examine the history and legacy of *Stepford* and its associated universe. Chapter 5 examines the three made-for-television sequels to *The Stepford Wives: Revenge of the Stepford Wives*, *The Stepford Children*, and *The Stepford Husbands*. These spin-offs have been almost entirely overlooked critically and academically. Their plot-lines are rather unsophisticated and they follow much more predictable horror genre trajectories. However, there is much to be gained from an analysis of these texts, particularly from a socio-cultural perspective. *Revenge of the Stepford Wives* offers a poignant critique of the use of tranquilisers and antidepressants as a solution to women's supposedly inherently neurotic tendencies, and the role of psychotropic drugs in maintaining myths about domestic bliss. *The Stepford Children* centres on themes of patriarchal rage, interrogating paternity and its relation to patriarchal domination. *The Stepford Husbands* flips the gender power dynamics of the original film and book, but in doing so presents an unsubtle example of backlash against feminism. Importantly, this gives context to the narrative choices of Oz's reimagining of *The Stepford Wives*, which is fundamentally an endorsement of some of the most salient themes of postfeminism in the early 2000s. Frank Oz's remake – the focus of Chapter 6 – is critically examined from a feminist perspective. Of importance is the way the film lampoons the original text, rendering it both an exemplar of postfeminist sensibilities and a flippant exercise in hyperbole and the carnivalesque – a far cry from the disturbing, slow burning horror of the original narrative. Finally, Chapter 7 will examine the legacy of *The Stepford Wives* in relation to contemporary imaginings of robot women, focusing primarily on *Ex Machina* and *Westworld*. Further, this chapter moves beyond fiction to look at Stepford wives in the real world – specifically the development of artificially intelligent sex dolls and robots. Of particular focus are the social implications of deep machine learning and human-machine intimacy in the context of ubiquitous computing. The chapter will question how progressively seamless interactions between humans, hardware, and software will influence perceptions of intimacy with robots and AI in the future.

****

The Stepford Wives opens with protagonist Joanna Eberhart (Katherine Ross) alone in an empty Manhattan apartment. The camera lingers on jungle themed wall paper, then on Joanna as she does a final check of the cupboards before staring pensively out of a window at the urban milieu she is about to leave behind. Ambient sounds of city traffic – horns, sirens – noises from the 'urban jungle,' permeate the silence. Out on the street, Joanna joins her two children in the family's station wagon, parked against the kerb. As they wait for Joanna's husband Walter (Peter Matheson) to join them, a man carrying a nude mannequin with a white cloth concealing its face crosses a busy intersection in front of them. Joanna, a talented photographer, quickly grabs her SLR camera to capture the action. What she cannot know, is that the scene offers an ominous foretelling of what is about to happen to her following the family's relocation to the lush, middle-class suburban town of Stepford, Connecticut.

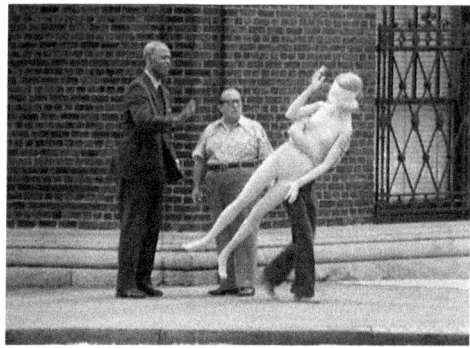

Figure 1: An ominous forewarning

offers an ominous foretelling of what is about to happen to her following the family's relocation to the lush, middle-class suburban town of Stepford, Connecticut.

It is evident from the outset that it is Walter's decision to move to Stepford. As Joanna later remarks, 'You pretend we decide things together, but it's always you, what you want. Why bother asking at all?' However, Walter does not just exploit his patriarchal privilege to get what he wants; he is also a self-centred and cunning liar. Walter claims not to know anyone in Stepford, but it is evident from the start that Walter does in fact know at least one person in town. His new neighbour Ted van Sant (Joseph Sommer) and he immediately becomes enmeshed with the local Men's Association: a tight knit, highly secretive male-only fraternity that meets every night in a large gothic mansion. Hence, it seems that the relocation to Stepford has been planned in advance.

Head of the Men's Association is a creepy, Lord Ruthven-like character called Dale 'Diz' Cobra (Patrick O'Neal) – a former Disney animatronics expert with a PhD from Berkley who likes to 'watch women do little domestic chores.' Other members include Ike Mazzard (William Prince) a sketch artist famous for his drawings of women, and Claude Axhelm (George Coe) – a linguistics expert who claims to be developing voice mapping software that will eventually function as a form of 'geographical' fingerprinting. What Joanne does not realise, until it is too late, is that Stepford is a town where men bring their wives to have them murdered and replaced with bespoke android replicas – subservient automations with idealised bodies that are always available for sex and do nothing but cook and clean: robots with the conversational repertoire of a spray starch advertisement – a dramatic departure from the intelligent, educated, pro-feminist women they replace.

The Stepford Wives presents a chilling portrayal of the way systems of patriarchal power operate to maintain the *status quo* on an individual and collective level, the man-made robot woman being the ultimate articulation of such machinations. Therefore, while the intention of this book is to pay homage to *The Stepford Wives*, it also goes far beyond this to offer a commentary on the *Stepford* universe as a whole, and to contextualise it in broader histories (and futures) of artificial women.

Chapter I: *The Stepford Wives*, Levin and the Gothic

Before looking in detail at *The Stepford Wives*, it is important to establish its history in the context of Levin's work more broadly – especially his use of the gothic: a style of horror concerned with psychological fear, foreboding places, isolation, entrapment and deceit. By the time Levin wrote *The Stepford Wives* he had established critical acclaim. Levin's Edgar Award-winning first novel *A Kiss Before Dying* (1953) was adapted to screen soon after its release in 1956 (directed by Gerd Oswald) and again in 1991, this time directed by James Dearden (who had earlier written the screenplay for the now infamous *Fatal Attraction* – directed by Adrian Lyne, 1987). However, it is Levin's second book *Rosemary's Baby* (1967) that cemented his prominence as a writer. The novel achieved enormous commercial success as did the film version, released in 1968, directed by Roman Polanski. Polanski's *Rosemary's Baby* received universal critical acclaim at the time and in 2014 was recognised for its heritage value and cultural significance by the American Library of Congress's National Film Registry. *Rosemary's Baby* introduces a number of important themes relevant to *The Stepford Wives* – in particular a focus on female subjectivity and questions of women's autonomy in relation to their bodies in patriarchal society. *Rosemary's Baby* is also heavily saturated with the gothic. This chapter will explore the significance of the gothic and its subclasses to *The Stepford Wives* (both Levin's novel and the film).

The Uncanny and the Gothic

In a 1992 interview with Suki Sandler, for the American Jewish Committee Oral History Library, Levin concedes that a strong adolescent interest in mystery and suspense stories, as well as movies based on the classic gothic tales *Dracula* (Stoker, 1897) and *Frankenstein* influenced his writing considerably. It is perhaps unsurprising then, that Levin's novels, along with their film adaptations, are imbued with the traditions of gothic fiction. The gothic is particular in that it elicits a certain kind of horror – a pervasive sense of dread and discomfort that finds origin in the uncanny, which is, in turn, best described as a feeling of trepidation accompanied by a peculiar, dream-like quality of something fleetingly recognisable in what is evidently unknown, conjuring an impression of *déjà vu*. The uncanny has to do with uncertainty, particularly in relation to what is being experienced. It involves an invasive sense that things – people, places, and objects – are not how they have come to appear through habit and familiarity (Royle 2003, pp.1-2; Punter, 2007, p.131). The catalogue of motifs, fantasies, and phenomena attributed to the uncanny are extensive, extending from corpses, dismembered limbs, and severed heads, to the thought of being buried alive – an anxiety commonly associated with catalepsy in gothic fiction, particularly the work of Edgar Allan Poe. Ghostly apparitions, madness, anthropomorphism, and doubt over whether an animate object is really alive or conversely, if a lifeless object, such as a doll or an automation, is actually living also fall under the broad range of what constitutes the uncanny (Jentsch, 1906, pp.221-7; Freud, 1919, pp.232-45).

Psychiatrist Ernst Jentsch was the first to explore the psychological underpinnings of this eerie phenomenon in his 1906 paper 'On the Psychology of the Uncanny,' though Sigmund Freud's 1919 essay 'The Uncanny' is usually associated with the term (Lindop, 2014). Jentsch describes the sensations of the uncanny, where feelings of 'new/foreign/hostile' overlay physical associations of 'old/known/familiar,' as *unheimlich* ('unhomely' in German). The *unheimlich*, which sits in direct opposition to the *heimlich* (homely), equates to a situation where someone feels 'not quite at home' or 'ill at ease' (Jentsch 217-19). These sensations are powerfully conveyed through the use of visual motifs in Forbes' *The Stepford Wives*, ominously foretelling that things are not what they seem: The man carrying a nude, faceless, female mannequin across a busy New York intersection in the opening sequence; an external shot of the family's station wagon travelling through the countryside on its way to Stepford and in the foreground, a graveyard full of large grey headstones that dominate the frame; an extended shot of a dead rodent floating in a pond as Joanna talks to her psychiatrist about her fears; the mysterious interaction between Walter and Ted Van Sant where Walter comments to Ted that his wife Carol 'cooks as good as she looks' (Carol had earlier presented Walter with a casserole), even though Walter claims not to know anyone in Stepford. Sensations of uncanniness are further compounded by Walter's ongoing lies, the overstated creepiness of Dale Cobra and the oddness of the Stepford residents in general, including the children on the school bus, who are unmistakably similar to the alien possessed children in Wolf Rilla's 1960 sci-fi horror *Village of the Damned*. Then there are the wives of Stepford themselves with their flattened affect and single-minded obsessions with polishing floors, ironing, and baking. The minimalistic, off-kilter sound score composed by Michael Small – well known for his compositions for thrillers including *Klute* (Alan J. Pakula, 1971), *Child's Play* (Sidney Lumet, 1972), and *Marathon Man* (John Schlesinger, 1976) – further contributes to the pervasive sense of *unheimlich* that permeates *The Stepford Wives*.

Jentsch attributes sensations of the uncanny to psychical resistances that emerge in relation to mistrust of the innovative and the unusual – 'to the intellectual mystery of a new thing' (1906, p.218): an emotional state that finds origin in the historical period of the Enlightenment. According to Terry Castle (1995, pp.8-10), it is the transformations of the 'age of reason,' with its rejection of transcendental explanations, valorisation of reason over superstition, aggressively rationalist imperatives, and compulsive quests for knowledge that first generated human experiences associated with the uncanny. In this sense, the eighteenth century 'invented' the uncanny (Castle, 1995, p.8). Freud builds on Jentsch's theory of the *unheimlich* by focusing on the *heimlich*, arguing that the term incorporates two sets of ideas. The heimlich can refer to what is familiar and agreeable, or it can mean 'what is concealed and kept out of sight' (1919, pp.234-5). In regard to the latter notion, the unheimlich denotes 'that which ought to have remained secret or hidden but has come to light' (Freud, 1919, p.225). Therefore, for Freud, who was primarily concerned with the latent content of the psyche, feelings of uncanniness emerge when dark, disturbing truths that have been repressed and relegated to the realm of the unconscious resurface, making their way abstractly into consciousness, creating an odd impression of the known in the unknown. According to Freud and Jentsch, the uncanny is epitomised in E. T. A. Hoffman's classic tale *Der Sandmann*. Here, the protagonist Nathaniel becomes infatuated with a strange girl called Olympia – the 'daughter' of his physics professor, Dr Spalanzani. Olympia is an automaton: an uncanny looking clockwork doll, artfully crafted from wood and wax. However, in a delusional break with reality, Nathaniel sees Olympia as a living person –

vibrant, cognisant, and reciprocal to his feelings. The dramatic realisation that she is a contrivance proves too much for Nathaniel to reconcile. He becomes violently psychotic, eventually throwing himself off a building. While fictional imaginings about artificial women coming to life date back to antiquity with tales like Pygmalion, from Ovid's *Metamorphosis*, the story of Nathaniel's obsession with Olympia is an important precursor to more modern imaginings about female androids, including *The Stepford Wives*; a subject that will be explored in detail in Chapter 2.

Just as the eighteenth century invented the uncanny (Castle, 1995, p.8), so too did it conceive the gothic, which, like other associated genres/styles of fiction, operates as a barometer for the anxieties plaguing a certain culture at a particular moment (Russ, 1973, p.260). The gothic novel emerged at a time when the industrial revolution was radically transforming social structures. Shifts from agriculture to industry meant a steady movement of population from rural areas to crowded urban centres. According to David Punter and Glennis Byron (2004, p.20), increased regimentation and mechanization of factory life divorced workers from the natural world, creating sensations of isolation and alienation that find expression in the gothic. Gothic fiction originates with the works of authors including Horace Walpole (*The Castle of Otranto*, 1764), William Beckford (*Vathek*, 1786), Matthew Lewis (*The Monk*, 1796) and the female-centred gothic romances of Ann Radcliffe, who wrote several multi-volumed novels, the most influential being *The Mysteries of Udolpho* (1794). Central to these classic gothic texts are themes involving isolation, entrapment, haunted places, and perfidious people who are not what they seem. The work of Radcliffe also explores the psychological and social experiences of women, particularly in relation to their disempowerment within patriarchal dynastic structures (Soare, 2010, p.89; Tay, 2010, p.264). Radcliffe's fiction, along with the work of nineteenth-century writers like Charlotte Brontë, is central to the more modern tradition of the female gothic – a term first used by Ellen Moers in 1976 to describe gothic texts that articulate women's dissatisfaction with patriarchal society, including fears of entrapment inside the domestic and within the female body. Though Moers defines the female gothic as exclusively the work of women writers (1976, p.90), it is a style that has long been appropriated by male authors too (Smith and Wallace, 2004, p.1), Levin included.

The Female Gothic

Daphne du Maurier's 1938 novel *Rebecca* is considered to have initiated the modern, female gothic (Doane, 1987, p.123), which became popular in the 1940s: undoubtedly, in part, due to the success of Alfred Hitchcock's screen adaptation of *Rebecca* in 1940, followed by a number of other cinematic reworkings of female gothic novels and plays including George Cukor's 1944 rendering of Patrick Hamilton's 1938 play *Gaslight*, Jacques Tourner's *Experiment Perilous* (1944), which originated as a novel by Margaret Carpenter (1943), and Joseph L. Mankiewicz's 1946 screen adaptation of Anya Seton's *Dragonwyck* (1944). Narratives of this style follow a similar plot structure: A young, inexperienced, and/or naïve woman falls in love with (and marries) a brooding, mysterious, superficially charming older man, only to discover that he is not what he seems. Invariably she finds herself alone in a large, foreboding house with her new husband, who becomes increasingly sardonic and contemptuous towards her. The focus is on the heroine's inner turmoil as her sense of self and her interpretation of the events unfolding around her are challenged. Confused about what is real or in her imagination, her attraction for her husband gradually becomes permeated by fear and repulsion. She is not sure if he loves her, hates her, is using her, is trying to drive her insane, or is trying to kill her (Russ, 1973, pp.667-8; Tay, 2003, p.265). In the majority of female-centred gothic texts, the heroine's suspicions about her derisive husband are confirmed (*Rebecca* being a rare exception). While this is often reliant on the corroboration of a male in a position of authority – a detective, psychiatrist, or medical doctor – in many instances, particularly in later tales, such as *Sudden Fear* (written by Edna Sherry, 1948, and adapted for cinema by David Miller, 1952), the heroine actively confirms her suspicions that her husband is trying to murder her *vis-a-vis* her own detective work. Furthermore, she often outsmarts him, beating him at his own game without any intervention from a male hero.

The overarching narrative structure of *The Stepford Wives* bears a close relationship to that of the classic female gothic. Joanna gradually realises that the man she has married is not what he seems. As his attitude towards her grows increasingly intolerant and belligerent, she comes to realise that he is a duplicitous monster and that she is alone and isolated in a town full of robots and murderous misogynists.

The film climaxes with a classic gothic sequence. In the middle of a dramatic electrical storm, Joanna finds herself trapped in a foreboding mansion – the Men's Association. The place is in darkness and abandoned, except for the vampiric Diz, who lures Joanna deep into the bowels of the building with a tape recording of her children crying. Unable to escape through the maze of dead end passages and empty rooms, Joanne eventually comes face-to-face with her worst nightmare – her robotic doppelgänger sitting at a dressing table in a strange giant 'doll's house' version of her own bedroom.

Levin locates his heroines in the tradition of the female gothic in his earlier texts too. His first novel, *A Kiss Before Dying*, is a compelling thriller crafted in the tradition of the gothic, but infused with elements of slick, tightly constructed hard-boiled detective fiction of the kind produced by authors such as Raymond Chandler and James M. Cain. The book is divided into three sections titled Dorothy, Ellen, and Marion: the first names of three daughters of a wealthy copper mine magnet called Leo Kingship. The villain (who remains unnamed until mid-way through the narrative) is a good-looking, smooth talking lothario, intent on leeching onto the Kingship fortune. In part one, he strategically targets Dorothy Kingship – a quiet, 'love-starved' college student whose favourite novel is *Rebecca*. However, his plans go wrong when she becomes pregnant. Rightly believing that her strict, uncompromising father will disown her under such circumstances, leaving the villain burdened with a penniless wife and child, he resorts to murdering her. In part two, the gold digger (later revealed to be a man called Bud Corliss) is now the boyfriend of Ellen Kingship. Ellen has adopted the role of private detective to investigate her sister's death, which authorities have wrongly ruled a suicide. But Ellen is too effective at the job. With the assistance of Dorothy's ex-boyfriend, who had seen the killer with Dorothy on multiple occasions, Ellen comes dangerously close to discovering the truth about Bud – so he murders her too. In part three, Bud shifts his attention to the final Kingship heiress, Marion. While Marion is oblivious to Corliss's sinister intents, Ellen's friend Gordon, who has taken over the role of detective following Ellen's demise, relentlessly pursues, and eventually exposes Bud's treachery to the remaining Kingship family members.

Rosemary's Baby and the Gothic

Levin's second novel, *Rosemary's Baby*, is far less hard-boiled and significantly more replete with the tropes and traditions of the gothic: foreboding buildings with dark, sinister histories; strange accidents and unexplained deaths; wild hallucinogenic dreams that are too visceral to be fantasy, yet too bizarre to be real; handsome husbands behaving very oddly; neighbours who are not what they seem; and further references to du Maurier – this time her 1965 novel *The Flight of the Falcon*. *Rosemary's Baby* adopts the subjective point-of-view of the protagonist, Rosemary Woodhouse (a stay-at-home wife who is estranged from her strict Roman Catholic family because they do not approve of her marriage to Guy), a protestant with a twice divorced mother. Central to the narrative is the setting: The Bramford apartment building – an imposing structure colloquially known as 'The Bram' (in evident homage to the author of *Dracula*). Rosemary is especially thrilled to be moving into the iconic Bramford, with its grotesque stone creatures crouching on the external walls and sub-divided apartments with high ceilings and ornate Victorian fixtures within. While Guy seems relatively *nonchalant* about the move, Rosemary's substitute father figure Hutch is horrified, cautioning them about the building's dark past and its insalubrious residents: two 'proper' Victorian sisters with a penchant for cooking and eating children, a witchcraft practitioner who conjured up the living Satan, an unidentified dead baby found abandoned in the basement, and curiously high rates of accidental deaths and apparent suicides.

Adding to the oddities of the building is the Woodhouse's strange, flamboyant elderly neighbours Minnie and Roman Castevets. The suicide death of the Castevets' 'adopted daughter' just days after Rosemary and Guy move in further reinforces Hutch's claim that the Bramford is a 'danger zone' (1967, p.13). Guy soon becomes especially friendly with the Castevets, visiting them often (much more so than Rosemary) and it is around this time that Guy, a professional actor, secures a prestigious role after his rival inexplicably succumbs to sudden blindness. Soon after, Rosemary becomes pregnant following a violent and vividly hallucinogenic encounter with what seems to be Guy – except with leathery skin, yellow eyes, and an extraordinarily large penis: a happening predicated by the consumption of some excellent, but chalky tasting mousse supplied by Minnie.

Rosemary's early pregnancy is difficult. She is wracked with chronic pain and excessive weight loss. When she does eat, she ravages raw meat. Throughout this time, Guy becomes progressively elusive and disengaged. Rosemary identifies a growing disparity between what he says and how he behaves. Others around her seem odd too. Her obstetrician Dr Sapirstein (recommended by the Castevets) is strangely unconcerned about her condition, insisting that she take the daily herbal 'remedies' diligently supplied by Minnie. Then Hutch collapses into a coma. Rosemary later discovers that he was planning to give her a book, *All of Them Witches*, which is passed on to Rosemary after Hutch dies. Through reading the book and discovering the satanic ancestry of Roman Castevets, Rosemary becomes a detective in the mystery of her pregnancy, except that what she is investigating seems too outlandish to be taken seriously. It appears as though Rosemary has become unhinged, suffering from some form of psychosis. Rosemary's experiences of birth are equally unreal – drugged and incapacitated, she is victim to the often over-clinicalised practices of modern scientific medicine.

When she regains consciousness, she is told that her baby is dead and then promptly injected with even more drugs after accusing Guy and Dr Sapirstein of lying. Later Guy assures her: 'You were crazy [...]. You were really ka-pow out of your mind. It happens in the last couple of weeks [...]. Prepartum I-don't-know, some kind of hysteria. You had it, honey, and with a vengeance' (1967, p.207). But Rosemary was/is not insane and her baby is not dead. Rosemary tracks down her baby, finding it hidden in the Castevets' apartment. She has been betrayed by Guy and her devil worshipping neighbours in the secret pact that involved her body, but not her. In a final narrative twist, Rosemary embraces her 'devil's child' with his eyes 'all goldenyellow, with vertical black-slit pupils' (1967, p.220), his buds of horns, tail, and clawed hands. In a sense, she has the last laugh.

Rosemary's Baby was published at a time when feminists were becoming increasingly critical of the various ways women's bodies were treated by a medical system dominated by patriarchy. As Barbara Ehrenreich and Deidre English argue, women invariably found themselves subject to insensitive and hazardous treatments: 'unnecessary hysterectomies, over-medicated childbirth, involuntary sterilisations, insufficiently tested contraception, and the almost universal condescension of male doctors' (2010, p.8). Women who asked too many questions or insisted, for example on a 'natural' childbirth, frequently found themselves labelled on their medical records as uncooperative or neurotic. Furthermore, serious complaints were likely to be dismissed as 'psychosomatic and attributed to women's assumed suggestibility' (2010, p.8).

In the late 1960s and early 1970s, underground publications like the 1970 booklet *Women and Their Bodies* – later published commercially in 1973 by the Boston Women's Health Book Collective as *Our Bodies, Ourselves* – were putting women's health in a radically new political and social context. Levin's novel can be readily situated in this cultural climate as a critique of patriarchal clinical practice, not in the least because Levin's wife was pregnant when he wrote *Rosemary's Baby* and he was likewise looking through the books she was reading on expectant motherhood. As Levin makes clear in his interview with Sandler (1992, p.34), *Rosemary's Baby* is not about a neurotic or delusional woman mistaking experiences of prepartum psychosis and postpartum depression for reality. On the contrary, Rosemary is absolutely right. What Rosemary experiences is the immediate terror of patriarchal control over women's bodies and minds as her husband sequesters her womb, using it as a tradable commodity for his personal benefit and gain.

In commentary originally appearing as an afterword to the 2003 New American Library edition of the novel, Levin describes how he was struck one day by the thought that a foetus could be an effective device for horror if the reader knew it was growing into something malignly different from the baby expected: 'Nine whole months of anticipation, with the horror *inside* the heroine!' (Levin, 2003, p.6). When Levin decided to write the novel, he concluded that the foetus could not be a genuine medical horror as this was hardly the stuff of popular fiction. Instead, his unfortunate heroine had to be impregnated either by an extra-terrestrial or the devil. Since John Wyndham's *The Midwich Cuckoos* (1957) had already explored the idea of women impregnated by aliens, Levin went with the devil (though he makes it clear that he does not believe in this concept at all). Over fifty years on from the publication of *Rosemary's Baby* and Polanski's film adaptation of the novel, it is easy to forget the significance of this plot choice and its role in initiating a cultural 'satanic zeitgeist.' Levin has stated that he feels the novel, and more so the film, played a major part in the popularisation of the occult, witchcraft, and Satanism: 'I mean all these people who hear backwards messages in song lyrics and stuff like that – I really feel a certain degree of guilt about having fostered that kind of irrationality' (Levin in Sandler, 1992, p.35).

The Urban Gothic

Another formative aspect of *Rosemary's Baby* is the setting. Central to the gothic is the subject of confinement and entrapment (both physical and psychological); this makes places terribly important. In classic gothic fiction, rambling castles, crumbling abbeys, and convents in isolated, foreign lands are preferred locations. However, in *Rosemary's Baby*, Levin takes the castle, divides it into a multi-residential apartment block, and situates it in the heart of Manhattan. Polanski's film version aptly uses the exterior of the iconic Dakota Apartments as a backdrop. It seems that Levin, a New York native, may have also had this well-known nineteenth-century building in mind when he imagined The Bramford, given the Dakota's imposing exterior, gothic revival architecture, lofty ceilinged dwellings overlooking a private central courtyard, and myths of ghostly encounters and curses – lore later bolstered by the 1980 murder of resident John Lennon on its doorstep.

The choice of urban settings as a site of uncanny horror first emerged in the Victorian era. According to Punter and Byron (2004, pp.26-8), what has become known as the 'Victorian gothic' is marked primarily by the domestication of gothic figures, spaces, and themes. Here, the exotic and historical settings that serve to distance horrors from the world of the reader in classic gothic fiction are replaced with more disturbingly familiar domestic locations and the urban landscape. The city, with its dark, narrow, winding streets and hidden byways supplant the labyrinthine passages of the earlier castles and convents as a liminal space – the 'other' that lies between the known and the unknown. The gothic villain is transformed too, as aristocrats and monks give way to madmen and scientists (Robert Louis Stevenson's 1886 novel *The Strange Case of Dr Jekyll and Mr Hyde* is one prominent example).

Punter and Byron (2004, p.26) contend that the domestication of the gothic is partly due to its appropriation by the sensation novel. Emerging in the 1860s and founded on three texts – *The Woman in White* (Wilkie Collins, 1860), *East Lynne* (Ellen Wood, 1861), and *Lady Audley's Secret* (Elizabeth Braddon, 1862), gothic sensation fiction focuses on the bourgeois world and is characteristically preoccupied with family secrets, domestic crime and disorder. Gothic sensation novels often emphasise a heroine entrapped in the home or some kind of institution and pay particular attention to questions of identity, sanity versus insanity, and female inequality in patriarchal systems of power, especially in regard to legal systems that benefit bullying, deceitful husbands (as in *The Woman in White*, for example). In other gothic sensation novels female transgression becomes particularly central. Here women tend to assume the role of both heroine and monster (Punter and Byron, 2004, p.27). For instance, in the acclaimed *Lady Audley's Secret*, the protagonist, Lucy Graham is a murderous adulterer who 'deserts her child, pushes husband number one down a well, thinks about poisoning husband number two and sets fire to a hotel in which her other male acquaintances are residing' (Showalter, 1983, p.163).

Sensation novels transformed the gothic by locating mysteries and horror in relatable spaces. As Henry James writes in reference to Wilkie Collins's 1866 novel *Armadale*, 'Instead of the terrors of "Udolpho," we are treated to the terrors of the cheerful country-house and the busy London lodgings. And there is no doubt these were infinitely the more terrible' (*The Nation*, 1865). The urban gothic provides a space where the tradition of the gothic can persist, but in a form that speaks back to the relevant social and political climate of the stories' creation. By setting *Rosemary's Baby* in a rambling apartment building in the heart of a densely populated, fast-paced metropolis, the source of terror is not a single known enemy, but potentially everyone. Sensations of isolation come not from nature and rural desolation, but from a pervasive sense of detachment unique to living in an overcrowded, hostile, modern urban environment.

Levin returns to these themes in his 1991 book *Sliver* (adapted for cinema by Phillip Noyce in 1993). 'Sliver' refers to a high-rise constructed on a very narrow block of land. Like The Bramford, the sliver building (labelled by media as the 'Horror High-Rise') is an apartment complex in Upper East Side Manhattan infamous for its unusually high number of macabre and unusual deaths (despite the structure only

Figure 2: The gothic mansion

being a few years old). The sliver building is owned by Pete Henderson, a reclusive voyeur in his late twenties who has every room in the complex installed with audio-visual closed-circuit monitoring, which he obsessively scrutinises on multiple screens from an apartment on the thirteenth floor where he lives. Pete also has an Oedipal complex that manifests in murderous obsessions with women around the age of forty who resemble his deceased mother. New tenant and heroine of *Sliver* – Kay Norris – fits this criterion with uncanny likeness, thus becoming the latest subject of Pete's infatuation. *Sliver* was published just a year before the landmark 'fly-on-the-wall' show *The Real World* (MTV, 1992 –) first aired on television. *The Real World* is considered to represent the birth of reality TV, some nine years before the *Big Brother* phenomenon (Trigell, 1991, p.vii). As with many of Levin's novels, including *The Stepford Wives*, he effectively mobilises the rich traditions and stylistic histories of the gothic; prophetically relocating them in current and emergent socio-cultural contexts with compelling effect.

The Suburban Gothic

In the early 1970s, when Levin wrote *The Stepford Wives*, he had just moved back to New York City from a suburban town very much like *Stepford*. Though Levin claims that the ideas in the book did not consciously come from life in the suburbs, he doubts he would have written *The Stepford Wives* the way he did if he had not recently lived in a similar place (Sandler, 1992, p.45). Just as the urban gothic operates as a reaction to the *unheimlich* places and spaces of the city, so too can the suburban gothic be viewed as an articulation of anxieties to do with the uncanniness of those areas that exist in the liminal borderland between the urban and the rural.

The rise of the suburban gothic coincides with mass migration to the suburbs that took place in the decades following the end of WWII and the dramatic changes in lifestyle that resulted. Since then, the 'burbs have proven a fruitful setting for horror and gothic fictions exploring the malignant flipside to the pro-suburban rhetoric espoused by various agencies and industries vested in their propagation (Murphy, 2009, p.4). A foremost sentimentality of the suburban gothic is that suburban utopia is mere façade. The suburban gothic plays upon the lingering suspicion that even the most ordinary-looking neighbourhood, house, family, has something to hide: that no matter how peaceful and homely a place looks, it is only ever a moment away from a dramatic, often sinister incident. As Bernice M. Murphy asserts: 'In the suburban gothic, one is almost always in more danger from the people in the house next door, or one's own family, than from external threats. Horror here invariably begins at home, or at least very near to it' (Murphy, 2009, p.2). Arguably, there is no better summing-up of the suburban gothic, with its interest in uncanny contradictions and binary oppositions, than in the sublime opening sequence of David Lynch's 1986 film *Blue Velvet*. Set to Bobby Vinton's 1963 version of the song 'Blue Velvet', the viewer is presented with a succession of images signifying an idyllic American suburban life: white picket fences juxtaposed against bluer-than-blue skies; cheerful, friendly residents that you can trust; a safe, caring place for children; leafy streets and lush, flower filled gardens; a comfortable home to call one's own. But there are tensions – pressures building and festering out of sight and if one looks a bit closer, just beneath the surface, the place is writhing in a vile, sinister mass of violence and horror. These unspoken subterranean terrors contaminate the realm of the *heimlich*, creating a visceral sensorium of defamiliarisation that is amplified by filmic techniques like colour intensification and slow motion tracking. The suburban gothic nightmare is revealed as one where neighbours have dark secrets to hide. The suburb manifests into a place of entrapment and unhappiness; a claustrophobic breeding ground for dysfunctionality and abuse; a locale for mindless conformity and materialism; a site where the most dangerous threats come from *within* (Murphy, 2009, p.3). These are all themes that are pivotal to the horror of what is happening on a covert level in the affluent, idyllic suburban enclave of Stepford.[2]

Though the suburb was certainly not born in the 1950s, this era did see an unprecedented boom in suburban living. According to Murphy (2009, p.6), between 1948 and 1958 eleven million new suburban homes were established in the US, with 83% of all population growth occurring in the suburbs. Following the end of World War II, the country was suffering a severe housing shortage exacerbated by the large scale return of soldiers from Europe and the Pacific region, coupled with an unprecedented surge in birth rates. Rundown urban centres became chronically overcrowded, so much so that it was not uncommon for people to live in places like box cars and chicken coops. Conversely, there was a lot of land surrounding most cities and in the US in particular, planning laws were relatively lenient (Murphy, 2009, p.6). Hence, savvy entrepreneurs saw this as an opportunity to meet the overwhelming demands for housing by creating enclaves that promised space, tranquillity, and affordable home ownership.

Abraham Levitt and Sons are the most recognised developers of this era. The Levitts did not invent the business of building suburbs, nor were they the only companies creating them, but they did perfect the process and were responsible for the establishment of three sprawling enclaves – known as 'Levittowns' in Long Island, Pennsylvania, and New Jersey – which were constructed between 1947 and 1958. Levittown homes were simple, modern, fully equipped with the latest appliances, and spaciously located at sixty-foot intervals on flowing curvilinear streets devoid of through traffic. Levittown communities further boasted elementary schools, playgrounds, swimming pools, and shopping centres. Nonetheless, it was their slick building methods that were especially innovative. Borrowing from manufacturing techniques pioneered by Taylorism and Fordism, the Levitts devised a twenty-seven step construction process, whereby each team would complete a single stage before moving onto the next home, rather like a production line. This, coupled with the use of cheap, durable materials like asbestos sheeting, cladding, and shingles, made Levittown homes highly affordable: particularly in consideration of government subsidies, which provided cheap mortgages and healthy loan guarantees for builders (Galyean, 2015; Gans, 1982, pp.3-14).

However, these new modes of living were not without of criticism. As John Keats wryly comments in his 1956 book about American suburbs *The Crack in the Picture Window*: 'For literally nothing down – other than a simple promise to pay, and pay, and pay until the end of your life – you too, like a man I'm going to call John Doane, can find a box of your own in one of the fresh air slums we're building around the edges of American cities' (Keats, 1956, p.xi). Remarks such as this are well-founded. Entrepreneurs like the Levitt family may have perfected the suburb from an ideological design perspective, but as sociologist Herbert Gans (1982, p.14) points out, suburbs were plagued by pervasive homogeneity and imposed conformity, intensified by topographic layouts that lent to mutual goldfish bowl observation. Prospective Levittown buyers were carefully screened through processes of 'social filtering' (Gans, 1982, p.14). People with records of job instability, legal difficulties, emotional disturbance, or unkempt appearance were excluded and until non-discrimination laws were enforced, sales staff refused to sell to Black people (Gans, 1982, p.14; Galyean, 2015; Murphy, 2009, p.6).

Consequently, communities like Levittown were white, non-immigrant, and mainly aged under forty with young children. According to Gans (1982, p.22), the vast majority of Levittowners (seventy-five percent) could be considered lower-middle-class and most male workers were white-collar with a small percentage (around twenty-five percent) blue-collar. As Gans argues, this pronounced homogeneity violated the ideal of balanced community and diversity, created dullness through sameness, and made people callous of the poor, intolerant of racial diversity, and scornful of the elderly (Gans, 1982, p.165).[3] According to Murphy (2009, p.71), the sameness, blandness, and materialism propagated in the suburbs also made them a particularly dangerous place for stay-at-home wives and mothers. Betty Friedan is well known for undiplomatically describing the suburb as a 'comfortable concentration camp' (1963, p.307) – a prison in which millions of middle-class women found themselves trapped in as a result of a conspiracy to reinforce conservative domestic ideology (Friedan, 1963, p.307).

This plot finds origin in a post-World War II push to restore traditional patriarchal order and reboot the economy. During the war the need for domestic labour shifted into high gear, particularly following the bombing of Pearl Harbor. With most able-bodied men aged between eighteen and forty either enlisted or drafted to the military, marginal workers – including women – became the target of recruitment campaigns. According to Melissa Dabakis, eighteen million women in the US entered the workforce during the war, six million for the first time. Of those first time workers, a great deal were middle-class women who were groomed to participate in the labour force 'for the duration' (Dabakis, 1982, p.187). Hiring strategies assumed the temporary labour of middle-class housewives, the idea being that after the war, there would be a return to 'normalcy' and these women would re-enter the home to 'manage consumption' (Dabakis, 1982, pp.187-8).

Hence, post-1945 a new 'propaganda of traditionalism' emerged in media and advertising where femininity was rigorously linked to a totalising celebration of domesticity and family life (Lasch, 1997, p.105). As Friedan (1963, pp.15-17) argues, in the 1950s women learned that to be truly feminine they should not want careers, higher education, or political rights. This message was so powerful that by the end of the 1950s, the average age of marriage had dropped into the teens, the US birth rate was among the highest in the world, and fewer and fewer women were entering professional work (which mainly consisted of careers in nursing, teaching, social work). According to Christopher Lasch (1997, p.105), this socially constructed commemoration of domesticity was very much a twentieth-century innovation tied to both the phenomena of suburban migration and a recuperation of masculine agency temporarily immobilised during the war years. Hence, suburban migration both incentivised, and was driven by, this new celebration of domesticity that characterised post-war, middle-class culture. As Robert Beuka (2004, pp.151-2) maintains, the suburbs isolated women from political, social, and financial power, as well as segregating them from employment, education, and cooperative parenting, thus facilitating political pushes to get them into the domestic realm. It is not surprising that narratives about isolation, depersonalisation, and body replacement are such a significant trope in the suburban gothic.[4] Stepford may be more prestigious than the sprawling Levittown enclaves and its inhabitants of a higher, more educated class, but it is a suburban nightmare just the same. The 'modified' wives of Stepford are exemplars of the cult of domesticity – the ideal outcome of discourses of traditionalism that were so rigorously endorsed through popular media and consumer product marketing in the decades following the end of World War II. However, while *The Stepford Wives* articulates what Friedan describes as 'the problem that has no name' (1963, pp.15-32), the wives of Stepford are not just rendered robot-like by their circumstances, they are literally replaced by machines – sterilised, fetishised replications of their real selves. Hence, as much as *The Stepford Wives* is grounded in the traditions of the female gothic and the suburban gothic, so too does it find origin in gothic science fiction and the long histories of fictional imaginings about artificial women, particularly those that emerged with industrial development. This will be explored in the following Chapter 2.

Chapter 2: Automatons, Androids, and Stepford Wives

> Why? Because we can. We found a way of doing it and it's just perfect. It's perfect for us and perfect for you [...]. See, think of it the other way around. Wouldn't you like some perfect stud waiting on you around the house? Praising you? Servicing you? Whispering how your sagging flesh was beautiful, no matter how you looked? (Dale Cobra to Joanna Eberhart)

This extract from a conversation between Dale 'Diz' Cobra and Joanna in answer to her question 'why?', just before she is murdered and replaced by a one-dimensional replica of herself, is indicative of fictional imaginings about artificial women that date back to antiquity. A foremost example is Ovid's tale about Pygmalion, who, dissatisfied with actual women, sculpted his ideal partner out of ivory, before calling on the divine power of the goddess Venus to turn his artefact into a living being. While Pygmalion's object of desire is enlivened through supernatural forces rather than male mastery over technology, the myth sets the foundation for the idea that manmade artificial women are a superior substitute for the real thing – a ubiquitous and recurring trope in fictional narratives about replica woman that became increasingly popular from the early 1800s, when scientific rationality and industrialization was transforming the social organisation of everyday life.

Chapter 1 established *The Stepford Wives*, and Levin's work more broadly, in the rich traditions of gothic fiction that first emerged in the eighteenth century, when enlightenment thinking and increased emphasis on scientific method was destabilising ideas about the materiality of human life and the nature of existence. Particularly resonant to *The Stepford Wives* is the modern female gothic with its focus on women's subjective experiences in patriarchal society, along with the suburban gothic – a sub-genre that confronts romanticised notions of suburban bliss, exploring instead, its malevolent underbelly. But as much as *The Stepford Wives* is entrenched in these gothic sub-genres, the book and the film are also rooted in gothic science fiction, which involves the amalgamation of scientific experimentation and rationality with the rich, pre-existing traditions of classic gothic fiction; a merger associated with *Frankenstein*. Although Frankenstein's monster itself differs significantly to the wives of Stepford, themes of alchemy and scientific ascendancy over natural processes of life and death, which are central to *Frankenstein*, share much in common with *The Stepford Wives*. The purpose of this chapter is to situate *The Stepford Wives* in the context of gothic science fiction and broader historical imaginings about artificial women. Underpinning tales about female automatons and androids are real life inventions, scientific theories, and philosophy. The chapter will explore the significance of technological innovation and theoretical ways of thinking about the corporeal form in relation to tales about artificial women in literature and sci-fi cinema.

Early Automatons

Just as fictional imaginings about artificial people are centuries old, so too have inventors, engineers, and mathematicians been using available technologies to make and/or illustrate the construction of automata dating as far back as the start of the Common Era (CE). *The Pneumatics of Hero of Alexandria* (translated by Bennet Woodcroft in 1851) is one prominent example where numerous human and animal shaped automations powered by water, air, and steam are intricately detailed. There are many other early CE texts that describe automatons as well, including the ninth-century *The Book of Ingenious Devices* and Al-Jazari's *The Book of Knowledge of Ingenious Mechanical Devices* (1206), both of which offer extensive descriptions of automatons driven by motion, water and air pressure (Nadarajan, 2007; Bedini 1964, pp.24-42). By the fifteenth century, actual automata were being designed and constructed and by the sixteenth century, inventors were creating independently moving automatons – prior to this they were attached to larger devices like clocks. Two of the oldest examples are a mechanised monk, made from wood and iron and a lute-playing lady, both of which are believed to have been created by clockmaker and engineer Juanelo Turriano in the 1560s (Kang, 2011, p. 81). Leonardo da Vinci also designed and constructed several automata, including a walking lion for King Louis XII in the early 1500s. However, it is the automatons of the 1700s that are the most widely known and sensationalised. Minsoo Kang (2011, pp.104-6) describes how Jacques de Vaucanson (1709–1782) triggered a veritable mechanisation craze with three automatons that were initially displayed in Paris in 1738: the *'fluteur automate'* – a life size mechanical statue that performed a repertoire of tunes on a flute; a fife-and-drum player; and the most astonishing automation of the period – a mechanical duck that could flap its wings, drink water, swallow grain and (seemingly) defecate (Kang, 104). Following Vaucanson, in 1773–1774, Swiss inventors Pierre and Henri-Louis Jaquet-Droz, along with their collaborator Jean Leschot constructed a group of three impressive automatons: a writer, a draftsman, and a musician. The latter, a female figurine, not only played an actual miniature harpsicord with fully articulated fingers, but moved with the music and simulated breathing with rising and falling movements of the chest. Like Vaucanson's inventions, these creations were sent on tour all over Europe (Kang, 2011, p.106).[5]

There is clear lineage from these extraordinary machines of the 1700s to nineteenth-century fictional imaginings about automata. This is particularly evident in the work of E.T.A. Hoffmann, who makes direct reference to Vaucanson, as do other early authors of tales about automatons including l'Isle-Adam and E.E. Killett, who wrote the short story *The Lady Automaton* (1901). Both Hoffmann's *Die Automate* (1814) and his better known tale *Der Sandmann* examine the psychological consequences of a breakdown in the distinction between organic subjects and synthetic objects and the uncanny idea that an automaton might be so lifelike that it is mistakable for a living being. As explored in Chapter 1, the uncanny is very much about ambiguity, especially in relation to whether something is alive or not (Royle, 2003, pp.1-2). In his 1970 paper 'The Uncanny Valley', roboticist Masahiro Mori discusses the uncanny specifically in relation to robots – the modern descendants of the free moving automatons built in the seventeenth and eighteenth century. Mori theorises that the uncanny has to do with a loss of sense of affinity and is an integral part of human instinct designed to protect us from proximal sources of danger, like disease. If a healthy person abruptly dies or, alternatively, if an authentic looking object, such as a human limb (especially one that moves) is suddenly revealed to be artificial, then its veracity immediately evaporates, triggering a level of creepiness and repulsion likely to plummet the observer into the pit of 'uncanny valley.' However, if there is verisimilitude, if a robot is clearly a machine, or alternatively, if it is so humanlike as to be completely indistinguishable from its organic prototype (a state only possible in science fiction), then the unexpected sense of repugnancy accompanied by descent into the uncanny valley is less likely to occur (Mori, 1970, pp.98-100).[6] In *Der Sandmann*, it is precisely an unforeseen loss of affinity that sends Nathaniel insane. His friends do not like Spalanzani's harpsicord playing female automaton. They comment that they find Olympia quite eerie and prefer to avoid her. Knowing that she is made of wood and wax, they cannot understand how a 'sensible fellow' like Nathaniel can possibly 'loose his head' over the doll. But Nathaniel is under the complete delusion that Olympia is alive. Tell-tale signs of artificiality, like the iciness of her flesh, are overridden by imaginings of a beating pulse and animated conversation. But in an unannounced visit to Spalanzani's home to see Olympia, Nathaniel is violently confronted with the undeniable fact that she is a mechanisation. The trauma of this forced reality about his love interest sends Nathaniel's already disturbed mind over the edge, propelling him headlong into the nadirs of the 'uncanny valley.'

Sensations of uncanniness can also be triggered when things that are assumed to be inanimate inexplicably come to life. As Mori hypothesises: 'Imagine a craftsman being awakened in the dead of night. He searches downstairs for something among the crowd of mannequins in his workshop. If the mannequins started to move, it would be like a horror story' (Mori, 1970, p.100). Indeed, mannequins and dolls that become animate are a popular trope in the horror genre. The acclaimed anthology series *The Twilight Zone* (Rod Sterling, 1959-1964) is just one example where the limits between organic and synthetic are often manipulated to uncanny effect. 'Living Doll' (E126, 1963), 'The Dummy' (E98, 1962), and 'Caesar and Me' (E148, 1963) all feature disturbing dolls or ventriloquist dummies that are occupied by some kind of malevolent life force that results in them 'coming alive.' In 'The After Hours' (E34, 1960) a woman becomes trapped in a department store after closing. As she rushes from door to door, trying to escape, the store's mannequins come to life. However, following her initial terror, she remembers that she too is a mannequin and that her time in the 'real world' was just a temporary reprieve. The boundaries between organic and synthetic are blurred in such a way as to compel questions about what it means to be alive and what this says about our own sense of identity. Similarly, 'Lateness of the Hour' (E44, 1960) and 'In His Image' (E103, 1963) explore questions of corporeality and consciousness by adopting the subjective position of people who believe they are carbon-based, only to find, in dreadful moments of realisation, that they are in fact robots.[7]

Science, Electricity, and Rationality

Fictional explorations of the interrelationship between technological innovation and the disintegration of binaries between living and inert find origin in *Frankenstein*. Unlike in *Der Sandmann*, which is very much about the uncanniness of technologies already developed (in the form of exquisite automata), *Frankenstein* has a forward-thinking interest in the evolution of technology, the emergent potentialities and demands of progress, and theoretical questions about the essence of life. Hence, Shelley moves away from the realms of the traditional gothic to incorporate specific interests in science and technology into the gothic structure. As Sian MacArthur (2015, pp.2-3) argues, *Frankenstein* is a product of its environment, raising questions and concerns about the hybrid nature of existence in an era of rapid technological change. Stories such as *Frankenstein* are all about the fervour of doing something because technology makes it possible – because one can, irrespective of whether one should. As the quote at the start of this chapter reveals, this is a sentiment shared by Dale Cobra. Hence, in gothic science fiction a new kind of tyrant emerged and mad scientists like Victor became pivotal characters. As with classic gothic villains, the mad scientist is arrogant, narrow-minded, lacks compassion, and has total conviction that he is entitled to do whatever he pleases (just like former Disney animatronics virtuoso Dale Cobra). Citing MacArthur: 'Demonstrating an overwhelming thirst for forbidden knowledge, the mad scientist is often megalomaniacal and eccentric, charged with a sense of self-importance that often clouds and distorts his ability to work within the boundaries of logic and reason' (2015, p.25). Frankenstein 'births' his monster with no thought about ramifications. Upon animation, the creature is revealed to be hideous – eight feet tall, with watery pale eyes and yellow skin that barely covers the muscles and vessels underneath (Shelley, 1818, p.46). It is so physically revolting that it cannot integrate into society, as it so desperately longs to do. Similarly, the members of the Stepford Men's Association eventually lose all semblance of moral and legal integrity in their vainglorious mission to eradicate their fleshly, flawed wives and replace them with immaculate simulacra.

Other early works of gothic science fiction follow similar themes, provocatively pushing the boundaries of moral and social acceptability. For instance, *The Island of Dr Moreau* (H. G. Wells, 1896) and *The Strange Case of Dr Jekyll and Mr Hyde* both centre on the despicable acts of mad scientists who operate outside the boundaries of tolerability in narcissistic pursuit of their cause. As opposed to supernatural transformations of figures like Dracula, who readily morphs into various forms (wolves, bats), the changes experienced by the beast-folk (human-chimeras) in *The Island of Dr Moreau* are purely surgical in nature, accomplished through invasive and excruciatingly painful means – the handiwork of vivisector Dr Moreau. Operating as allegory for colonial supremacy, Wells' story draws on nineteenth-century theories of atavism and 'chromatics of race' notoriously proposed by Italian criminal anthropologist Cesare Lombroso, who maintained that physical characteristics like dark skin colour, high cheekbones, and prominent jaws were determinants of criminal and psychopathological behaviour – ideas that were extensively exploited to justify social Darwinism.[8] Similarly, *Dr Jekyll and Mr Hyde* explores the 'bestial' origins of civilised humans and the idea that criminals and the insane can be identified through tangible characteristics played out in the physical and behavioural metamorphosis Jekyll undergoes each time he transforms into the violent, murderous Hyde (Krumm, 1999, p.53).

Just as *The Island of Dr Moreau* and *The Strange Case of Dr Jekyll and Mr Hyde* are informed by scientific rationality of the time, so too is *Frankenstein* influenced by popular technical and medical thought, in particular prominent debates from the turn of the nineteenth century about the nature of life initiated by experiments in 'galvanic resurrection,' pioneered by Luigi Galvani. Though Shelley does not provide specific detail of how Frankenstein invigorates his monster, in her 1831 preface to the novel, she does describe Galvanism as having offered token to the possibility of a corpse being reanimated. Given public attention generated by dramatic displays of galvanic reanimation and the high profile discussions emerging from them by members of the British Royal College of Surgeons in the years leading up to the publication of *Frankenstein* (Ruston, 2005, p.75), it seems unlikely that questions raised in these deliberations, such as how to define life and how living bodies are different to dead or inorganic forms, did not impact on the writing of *Frankenstein*. Moreover, it is evident that these debates, coupled with feats of galvanic animation and the pervasive influence of Cartesian logic, inspired later fictions about the creation and animation of artificial women.

A number of media sources, including *Kirby's Wonderful and Eccentric Museum; or, Magazine of Remarkable Characters* (1803-1820), detailed Galvani's early experiments in animal and bio-electricity using dissected frogs legs and mechanically generated current, whereby he proposed that by exciting the positive fluid of the nerves, an animal could be bought to life. However, it was the research of Galvani's nephew Giovanni Aldini that had the greatest influence on both the medical community (especially in England) and on later fictional imaginings about (re)animation. From 1802-1803, Aldini gave a series of public lectures and performed a number of much publicised galvanic experiments in the name of scientific research. The first of these involved the dissected body of a freshly killed dog, which became wildly animated when subjected to electrical charge. Following this, Aldini electrically stimulated of corpses of recently executed criminals: legally permissible under the Murder Act of 1751 (Stephens, 2015, p.276). The first, and most widely reported display of galvanic human resurrection was performed on the body of George Forster, who was executed for drowning his wife and child in the New Canal at Paddington in January 1803. Before an audience that included members of the London Royal College of Surgeons, Aldini attached a number of electrodes to Forster's body, which became horridly contorted with electrical charge: As reported in an article titled 'Interesting Particulars of George Forster' (*Kirby's Wonderful and Eccentric Museum*, 1803, p.36): 'it appears that a hand of the deceased, was made to move, lift up, and clench the fist, and an eye seen to open, the legs and thighs set in motion; and all this, some hours after his death had been inflicted.'

One prominent argument fuelled by Aldini's high profile 'Galvanic Miracles' – as London's *The Morning Post* termed these demonstrations in an article published on the 6 January 1803 – was that of surgeon John Abernethy, who viewed galvanism as a 'very powerful means of resurrection in cases of suspended animation' under circumstances such as drowning, asphyxia, and apoplexy (loss of consciousness following a stroke or heart attack). Since the development of the static electricity machine by Otto von Guericke in 1672, there had been a progressive interest in the application of medical electricity for physical states such as paralysis and palsy, and later – following the invention of the Leyden jar by Pieter van Musschenbroek in 1745 – to conditions like melancholia (Beaudreau and Finger, 2006, pp.330-45; Locke and Finger, 2007, pp.257-70). In fact, as evidenced by articles in the *American Journal of Psychiatry*, electric shock treatment to the brain was readily used to treat clinical depression and schizophrenia well into the 1940s and 1950s, and is still sometimes used in limited situations (under sedation) today (Shorter and Healy, 2007).

However, it is Abernethy's more radical ideas (by contemporary standards) that are especially resonant to gothic science fiction and fantasies about machine animation. Influenced by the prominent theories of Cartesian dualism and mechanistic physiology conceived by René Descartes in the seventeenth century, Abernethy considered life to be separate from the physical arrangement of the body. For Descartes, human beings are an amalgam of two distinct elements: the body – an automation made of matter; and the uniquely human possession of a soul – an immaterial entity that provides consciousness, reasoned thought, and the ability to communicate (Kang, 2011, p.117). Similarly, Abernethy conceived that the dead state of the body is its natural one and that life is a substance that becomes 'superadded,' stopping it from decomposing and decaying as it would if left alone. He posited that the human body is composed of three separate but closely associated entities: physical organisation (muscles, fibres, nerves, and organs), the superadded substance 'life,' and the mind (intelligence, perception): 'in the human body there exists an assemblage of organs, formed of common inert matter, such as we see after death, a principle of life and action, and a sentient and rational faculty, all intimately connected, yet each apparently distinct from the other' (Abernethy, 1814, pp.77-8). It is worth noting that Abernethy's ideas did not go unchallenged. Surgeon William Lawrence (who was the Shelley family's doctor) publicly rejected the idea of life as a discrete and separate substance; instead he understood vitality as simply the working operation of all the body's functions as a sum of parts. However, this notion was rejected at the time for being too radical since it suggested the absence of a soul (Ruston, 2005, p.22).

Galvanic Miracles and Machine Women

Cartesian thinking involving references to the human body as a natural automation, vitalised by a soul and a mind, coupled with enlightenment notions about the power of electricity to provide mastery over these processes, has proven to be a seductive formula in stories about artificial women. A foremost fiction to indulge these ideas, and one especially important to *The Stepford Wives*, is *L'Eve Future*. As Mary Ann Doane comments, *L'Eve Future* is frequently cited as the exemplary forerunner of cinematic representations of mechanical women (2004, p.251). In *L'Eve Future*, the Pygmalion myth is enacted. Just as the men of Stepford find solution to the 'problem' of their imperfect, independently thinking wives through replication and replacement, so too is the human subject (a woman called Alicia Clary) in *L'Eve Future* seen as chronically defective by means of her personality and therefore in need of urgent substitution. As with the women of Stepford, every facet of Alicia's physicality is captured and duplicated – her movements, features, flesh, voice, and smell: All but her problematic 'soul.'

The central character in *L'Eve Future* is real life inventor Thomas Edison, whose actual achievements are fictionally extrapolated to phantasmagorical heights in the novel. Edison uses his mastery of electricity and the telephone create to an array of wondrous equipment in his pavilion at 'Menlo Park.' However, his pet project is the fabrication of the perfect imitation human being – an 'android' built using 'a combination of exquisite substances, elaborated by chemistry' (l'Isle Adams, 1886, pp.60-61). As an important side-note, the term 'android' originates in *L'Eve Future*. Prior to this, independently moving human replicas were invariably described as automata. Thus far, Edison has completed a 'magneto-electric entity' (l'Isle Adams, 1886, p.59) – a functioning female 'skeleton' of sorts, called Hadaly (which is said to mean 'ideal' in Iranian), along with a responsive female forearm and hand that exactly replicates a living limb in all respects (including core temperature). But it is the personal crisis of his aristocratic friend Lord Ewald that initiates the full development of a superlative artificial woman. Lord Ewald arrives at Edison's pavilion in a near suicidal state. He has fallen in love with Alicia, who looks exactly like the *Venus Victorious* (or *Venus Victrix*), but whose character (soul) is so 'flawed'– both intellectually and morally – that Ewald could 'gleefully throttle' her. Considering his friend's dilemma, Edison proposes a solution by creating an ideal replication of the real Alicia using the prototype Hadaly as a foundation:

> ...making use of modern science, I can capture the grace of her gesture, the fullness of her body, the fragrance of her flesh, the resonance of her voice, the turn of her waist, the light of her eyes, the quality of her movements and gestures, the individuality of her glance, all her traits and characteristics, down to the shadow she casts on the ground – her complete identity in a word. I shall be the murderer of her foolishness, the assassin of her triumphant animal nature. In the first place I will reincarnate her entire external appearance, which to you is so deliciously mortal, in an apparition whose human likeness and charm alone will surpass your wildest hopes, your most intimate dreams! And then, *in place of this soul which repels you in the living woman, I shall infuse another sort of soul* [original emphasis], less aware of itself [...], a soul capable of impressions a thousand times more lovely, more lofty, more noble. (l'Isle Adams, 1886, pp.63-4)

Though somewhat opposed at first, Ewald goes along with his friend's plan, which involves luring Alicia to the pavilion, where her voice will be recorded and her physical measurements noted. Then she will be discreetly anesthetised – without her knowledge – so that while unconscious, Edison can take moulds of her teeth and tongue, along with various 'transpirations' of her body from head to feet for the purpose of identifying and replicating her various 'perfumes' using chemical compounds. Following this, she will be replicated, part by part: dermis, epidermis, rosy mouth, pearly teeth, aroma, voice, sapphire eyes, movement, equilibrium, and disposition. Structurally, her facsimile will comprise of mechanised systems involving delicate steel wires, cylinders and 'flexions' couched in metal and plastics. Electrical currents powered by a miniature electro-magnetic motor and distributed throughout the body via an interlaced network of complex wires will serve as exact imitations of nerves, arteries and veins (l'Isle Adams, 1886, pp.130-164).

Using similarly clandestine methodologies, the men of Stepford aggregate data about their wives. Acclaimed sketch artist Ike Mazzard discretely draws Joanna, without her prior consent, as she circulates among the members of the Men's Association following their impromptu descent on the home under the guise of a committee

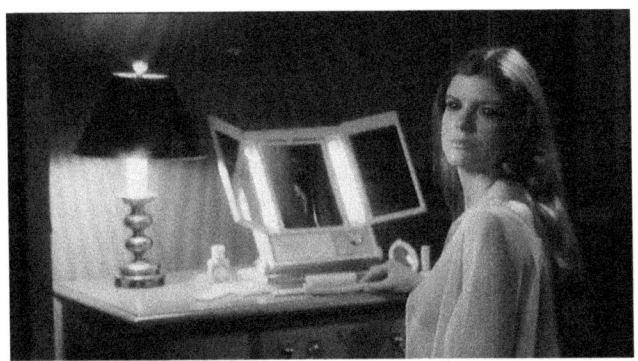

Figure 3: Joanna's doppelgänger

meeting. In the film, Joanna is initially flattered by the artist's rendition of her, but in Levin's book she becomes instantly uncomfortable when she realises what is happening: 'She felt suddenly as if she were naked, as if Mazzard were drawing her in obscene poses. She crossed her legs; wanted to cross her arms too but didn't' (Levin, 1972, p.33). The wives are then asked to participate in a project orchestrated by Claude Axhelm involving them recording extensive lists of words, syllables, and other personal information – where they were born, every place they have lived and for how long, lullabies they sing to their children, and any other information (all under the ruse of that their data will form some kind of geographical ethnography). Instead, this information is used to develop the vocal repertoire of the duplicate wives. While neither the novel nor the film detail the mechanics of the androids built at the Men's Association, the impetus and the outcomes are very similar to that described in *L'Eve Future*. The artificial women of Stepford are physically enhanced – they have bigger breasts, smaller waists, are perfectly made up, and smell nice. But importantly they also have their 'triumphant animal nature' murdered and replaced by far more amenable dispositions.

In *L'Eve Future*, Edison and Ewald spend much time philosophically contemplating the science of physiology and the mechanical nature of the body made popular by Cartesian philosophers like Descartes and Julien Offray de La Mettrie, a materialist thinker well known for his 1747 book *L'Homme Machine*, where he analogically likens the human body to machinery. Specifically, Edison employs the concept of the human form as a living automation to establish the idea that women are merely an assemblage of falsities and fakery: an accretion of wig work, greasepaint, pastes, lacquers, dentures, wadding, girdles, orthotics, synthetic perfumes, contrived glances, false smiles, and pretences of love. Edison further drives home his point by presenting a 'heliochromatic' moving image of a 'very pretty and quite youthful blonde girl' (l'Isle Adams, 1886, p.117) dancing and singing seductively. This vision is then replaced by one of a 'little bloodless creature, vaguely female in gender, with dwarfish limbs, hollow cheeks, toothless jaw with practically no lips, and almost bald skull, with dim squinting eyes, flabby lids, and wrinkled features, all dark and shiny' (l'Isle Adams, 1886, p.118), which Edison proclaims to be the same woman stripped of her cosmetic scaffold. His conclusion is that a replacement is a far more palatable option: 'Any woman of the destructive sort is more or less an Android, either morally or physically – in that case, one artifice for another, why not have the Android herself?' (l'Isle Adams, 1886, p.123).

The idea of femininity as a contrivance brings to mind Joan Riviere's 1929 paper 'Womanliness as Masquerade'. Here, Riviere proposes that femininity is sub-consciously assumed by women and worn as a mask in order to be successful in patriarchal society. The performance of womanliness functions as a way of distracting from attributes of intelligence and competence that might otherwise present a threat to masculinity. Hence, womanliness can be deployed as a strategy to avoid retaliation. Judith Butler's later work extends this argument. Drawing on Simone de Beauvoir's statement that 'one is not born, but, rather, *becomes* a woman' (de Beauvoir, 2009, p.172), along with Maurice Merleau-Ponty's account of the body as a 'historical idea' rather than a 'natural species' (Merleau-Ponty, 2012, pp.77-86), Butler argues that gender is a social construction that has been institutionalised and naturalised over time through a 'stylised repetition of acts' which the body is compelled to perform (Butler, 1988, p. 519). To be a woman (or a man), according to this distinction, is not a natural fact, but rather a sustained and constant corporeal accomplishment (Butler, 1988, p.522). Underpinning the performance of gender are power relations that have cultural survival as their end game. As Butler argues: 'gender is a performance with clearly punitive consequences. Discrete genders are part of what "humanizes" individuals within contemporary culture, indeed, those who fail to do their gender right are regularly punished' (1988, p.522). In texts like *L'Eve*

Future and *The Stepford Wives*, it is the perceived failure on the part of women to perform their gender, subject to tacit collective agreements about what constitutes femininity, which drives the misogynistic imperative to replace them with a version that does.

Another prominent text featuring the replacement of a biological woman with a mechanical copy using the marvels of science and harnessed electricity is Fritz Lang's German Expressionistic masterpiece *Metropolis* (1927). Metropolis is a futuristic megacity symbolic of industrialisation at a time of economic misery and rising fascism in Weimar-Republic Germany. The proletariat slog away in the grimy bowels of the 'Machine Hall' risking their lives operating the colossal 'Moloch Machine', while the bourgeoisies live high above the grind in a fantasy world of hedonism and excess. The stark contrast of these existences is fractured when the film's heroine Maria (Brigitte Helm) brings a group of children up from the ghetto to show them how their privileged 'brothers' live. She immediately captures the attention of Freder (Gustav Frohlich), the son of the city's founder Joh Fredersen (Alfred Abel), who becomes mesmerised by her. Venturing into the viscera of Metropolis in search of Maria, Freder experiences firsthand the true horrors of the worker's conditions and becomes a passionate advocate for their rights, much to the distain of his powerful father.

Determined to discredit the enigmatic Maria, Fredersen consults mad scientist and once rival Rotwang (Rudolph Klein-Rogge). Much like Edison in *L'Eve Future*, Rotwang has created a prototype android – a fully functioning metallic 'machine-man' – crafted in the image of his former lover Hel, who left him for Fredersen and died giving birth to Freder. Like Hadaly, the only thing missing from Hel are the fleshly outer layers required to pass her off a human. Fredersen demands that Rotwang give his machine-man the likeness of Maria with the idea of using the false Maria to sow discord between the workers, destroying their belief in their saviour. Rotwang agrees, but only because he sees it as an opportunity to devastate Fredersen, his city, and his son. Hence, Rotwang kidnaps Maria and confines her to the attic of his strange, asymmetrical laboratory/home in the heart of Metropolis. It is here that Rotwang performs a futuristic version of galvanic animation involving the transference of Maria's discrete life substances onto the mechanical Hel via electrical current channelled through a spectacular and complex system of wires, rods, conductor plates, and electrodes.

Whereas the real Maria is a saintly, Madonna-like activist calling for worker's rights through peaceful mediation, her doppelgänger is a lascivious seductress and destroyer – the 'whore of Babylon' riding on a seven headed beast who preaches of violent revolt and destruction of the city's machines. Therefore, while she is not a 'perfect woman' in the sense that Edison conceives the imitation Alicia or the Stepford husbands imagine their replica wives, the false Maria is nonetheless a hyper-sexualised product of masculine techno-creation reflective of a deep seated patriarchal desire to control women.

Historically, the thrill of mastery over science has been socially constructed as a masculine accomplishment. The ideological implications being that the connection between patriarchy and machines is natural: that there is an inherent biological tendency for men to be technologically minded. This myth is reinforced by dominant discourses that persistently associate masculinity with logic, rationality, and reason. Women, on the other hand, tend to be socially constructed as more emotional, less analytic, and closer to nature – the very thing that science seeks to dominate (Wajcman, 1991, p.137). By aligning women with nature and then further conflating them with technology, women and machine become meshed together into a common signifier of Otherness (Huyssen, 1981. P.226-8).

Mastery over technical innovation is rooted in the maintenance of patriarchal domination. In texts like *L'Eve Future* and *The Stepford Wives*, the replacement of 'problematic' organic women with entirely manageable facsimiles, presents a sadistic response of feelings of loss of patriarchal power. Sadism is characterised by a need for control. Rendering the sadist's object of desire powerless is fundamental to his/her basic aim (Socarides, 1974). Edison's scathing deconstruction of the female form has much to do with the fact that he has no control over the 'fakery' involved in womanly masquerade, as opposed to the artifice of the android, which, despite being as much of an imitative system as gender, is entirely regulated by him. Similarly, Cobra's cool contemplation of Joanna as she works in her kitchen and his cutting comment that he likes to 'watch women doing little domestic chores' are indicative of a sadistic desire to disempower her – reducing her to an object of fascination little different from the household appliances surrounding her.

The ability to control artificial women in the face of failure to manage their organic prototypes is played out in *Metropolis*, where the false Maria is burned at the stake and in *The Stepford Wives* where mechanical wives are installed in the home and supermarket – hence, machines and women are relegated to their 'proper' place (Doane, 2004, p.255). However, a fundamental difference between *The Stepford Wives* and the majority of stories about artificial women has to do with subjectivity. *The Stepford Wives* is entirely about Joanna's experiences and the horrific realisation that her husband secretly buys into systems of patriarchal privilege to the same extent as the other misogynistic men of Stepford. This is driven home in the final scenes of the film when Joanna is confronted by her doppelgänger, with its large synthetic breasts and vacant eyes. It is at this point that the true horror of Walter's desires is fully realised. *The Stepford Wives* pessimistically suggests that all heterosexual men want women that are fundamentally just sex robots.

Sci-Fi Cinema and Fembots

Sci-fi films date back to the beginnings of the moving picture with George Méliès' classic *Le Voyage Dans la Lune* (*The Voyage to the Moon*, 1902). However, sci-fi did not emerge as a distinctive film genre until the 1950s – an era that became known as the 'Golden Age' of sci-fi: so-called due to the sheer volume of sci-fi B-movies made in this decade (Sobchack, 2005, p.263). Sci-fi is imbued with allegory, functioning as a conduit for social and political tensions at a given point in time. The 1950s was an especially anxious era dominated by uncertainty about situations including the new Cold War, threat of nuclear annihilation, and corporate capitalism. Sci-fi cinema reflected these tensions. Films featuring giant and/or mutant insects and other creatures creating mass urban chaos like *The Beast from 20,000 Fathoms* (Eugène Lourié, 1953), *Them!* (Gordon Douglas, 1954) *Tarantula* (Jack Arnold, 1955), *The Beast with a Million Eyes* (Roger Corman, 1955), *The Deadly Mantis* (Nathan Juran, 1957), and *The Brain Eaters* (Bruno Vesota, 1958) articulated the threat of radiation and nuclear annihilation. Alien invasion films such as *The Day the Earth Stood Still* (Robert Wise, 1951), *Zombies From the Stratosphere* (Fred C. Brannon, 1952), *Invaders from Mars* (William Menzies, 1953), *It Came from Outer Space* (Jack Arnold, 1953), and *Invasion of the Body Snatchers* (Don Siegel, 1956) dramatized a fear of Communism and Cold War nightmares about being 'taken over' and ideologically brainwashed by powerful inhuman 'others' (Sobchack, 2005, pp.264-5; Vizzini, 2008, p.30). Films about battling the frontiers of outer space and staking new territory on other planets, for instance *Destination Moon* (George Pal, 1950), *Flight to Mars* (Lesley Selander, 1951), *Project Moon Base* (Richard Talmadge, 1953) and *Conquest of Space* (Byron Haskin, 1955), enforced ideologies of American imperialism and technological potency.

However, by the end of the 1950s the production of sci-fi feature films went into major decline. Partially, this had to do with the economic collapse of the monopolistic Hollywood studio system and block-booking practices that low-budget B-films and double features depended on (Sobchack, 2005, p.266). Television also began providing audiences with good quality major entertainment alternatives like *The Twilight Zone*, *The Outer Limits* (Showtime, 1963-9) and *Star Trek* (Gene Roddenberry, 1966-8). Sci-fi feature films certainly did not disappear during the 1960s, but there were significantly fewer made. Some well-known exceptions include Stanley Kubrick's *Dr. Strangelove: Or How I Learned to Stop Worrying and Love the Bomb* (1964), *Fantastic Voyage* (Richard Fleischer 1966), and *Planet of the Apes* (Franklin J. Schaffner, 1968). By the 1960s, anxieties had shifted too; living under the nuclear shadow had become normalised. Instead the new 'alien threat' came from counterculture movements and political activists calling for civil rights, female equality, gay rights, and an end to the Vietnam War. As Sobchack notes: 'the earthbound gravity of civil unrest, political assassinations, bloody demonstrations, interrogation of social institutions from government to the family, and the ambiguous and nonnuclear jungle war in South-East Asia belied high-tech SF fantasies about colonial expansion and American military pre-eminence' (2005, p.266). Adding to this, the reality of the 'space race' and the 1969 Apollo moon landing made the futurism of sci-fi with its outer space special effects seem outdated (though this changed around 1977 following the dawn of the blockbuster and the release of films like George Lucas' *Star Wars* and Spielberg's *Close Encounters of the Third Kind*).

The Stepford Wives

While fewer sci-fi films were being made in the 1960s to the mid-1970s in general, films involving AI and robot characters experienced a marked increase in popularity during this period. This was undoubtedly triggered by technological transformations taking place at the time, particularly in the domestic sphere where microcomputers (including Apple's 'All-In-One Personal Computer' and the 'Commodore Personal Electronic Transactor'), the Intel4004 Central Processing Unit (CPU), the programming language C, floppy disks, Atari game consoles, VCRs, digital wrist watches, portable cassette recorders, and (very cumbersome) digital cameras all became available to the public. These products radically transformed social and interpersonal relationships with technology. They also initiated a whole new set of possibilities and anxieties about the future of innovation. *Alphaville* (Jean-Luc Goddard, 1965), *2001: A Space Odyssey* (Kubrick, 1968), *Dark Star* (John Carpenter, 1974), and *Demon Seed* (Donald Cammell, 1977) focus on sinister AI supercomputers. *Dr. Goldfoot and the Bikini Machines* (Norman Tourog, 1965), *Dr. Goldfoot and the Girl Bombs* (Mario Bava, 1966), *THX 1138* (George Lucas, 1971), *Silent Running* (Douglas Trumbull, 1972), *Fantastic Planet* (René Laloux, 1973), *Westworld* (Michael Crichton, 1973) and its sequel *Futureworld* (Richard H. Heffron, 1976), *Star Wars*, *Alien* (Ridley Scott, 1979) and *Star Trek: The Motion Picture* (Robert Wise, 1979) all feature android characters of various kinds. In addition, television shows like *My Living Doll* (CBS, 1964-65), *Star Trek*, *The Twilight Zone*, *The Six Million Dollar Man* (ABC, 1974-78), *The Bionic Woman* (NBC, 1976-78) and *Battlestar Galactica* (ABC, 1978-79) are all replete with robots and AI. Indeed, it would be fair to say that something of a robot zeitgeist was occurring in this era.

In sci-fi, robot/AI characters are highly gendered and the way they are presented varies accordingly. Classically, male robots are coded as murderous, duplicitous, and a danger to human beings. This trope finds origin in Karel Capek's 1920 play *Rossum's Universal Robots* (*R.U.R.*). It is here that the term robot originates, as an adaptation of the Czech word 'robota' – meaning servitude or forced labour (Kakoudaki, 2014, p.9). *R.U.R.* has been, and continues to be, highly influential to the way robots and AI technologies are imagined. In mainstream media, technophobic stories about rogue automations are common, and in film and television, the once trusted AI robot/mainframe turned murderer is a popular theme. Alpha 60 in *Alphaville*, HAL9000 in *2001: A Space Odyssey*, Proteus IV in *Demon Seed*, Ash (Ian Holm) in *Alien*, The Gunslinger (Yul Brynner) in *Westworld*, ALEX7000 in *The Bionic Woman* ('Doomsday is Tomorrow, Pt 1 and 2,' 1977) and the machines in 'A Thing about Machines' (*The Twilight Zone* Season 2, Episode 4, date), are just a few examples from the 1960s and 1970s.

As noted, most often the seditious machine is gendered male, as is the case with Alpha 60, HAL, Proteus IV, Ash, ALEX7000, and The Gunslinger. This is not to say that subversive female machines do not exist – 'Mother' in *Alien* is one example of a villainous female gendered AI from this era, and there are many more in contemporary film and television as will be discussed in Chapter 7. But overwhelmingly, in the 1960s and 1970s (and before) artificial women were invariably created to be controlled by men. This includes killer 'fembots': a term that finds origin in *The Bionic Woman*. The fembots first appear in the three part, season two episode 'Kill Oscar' (Episodes 6, 7, and 8, 1977). Here, corrupt former Office of Scientific Intelligence (OSI) scientist Dr Carl Franklin (John Houseman) replaces the secretaries of prominent OSI employees with fembots in order to steal an experimental weather device for a foreign power. The fembots later appear in the season three, two part episode 'Fembots in Las Vegas' (episodes 3 and 4, 1978), where they are again deployed by Dr Franklin – this time to steal an energy ray weapon. Female robots are used in a similar, but tongue-in-cheek, way in *Dr. Goldfoot and the Bikini Machine*. Here, money hungry mad scientist Dr. Goldfoot (played by Vincent Price) creates an army of bikini-clad 'fembots' designed to seduce wealthy men into signing over their assets. In *Dr. Goldfoot and the Girl Bombs*, he uses his fembots to blow up high-ranking NATO generals, starting a war between Russia and the US.

Fembots, like other artificial women, can be interpreted as a masculine fantasy involving the reclamation of control over women by reducing them to their most manageable form. Female robots, on the whole, speak with particular intensity to anxieties, not only about women *per se*, but about the power of reproduction. As a number of scholars, including Doane (2004), Andreas Huyssen (1982), and Brian Easlea (1983) have argued, patriarchal drive for control over nature can be interpreted as a desire to appropriate female procreative powers, enacting the ultimate technological fantasy of creation without a mother. According to Easlea, science and the development of weapons are a form of patriarchal compensation for not being able to give birth to babies. Specifically, Easlea is referring to the nuclear arms race. For Easlea, it is not coincidental that the first uranium bomb to be dropped on Hiroshima was named 'Little Boy' (1983, p.5). With this in mind, it is perhaps unsurprising that fembots (in essence, female gendered weaponry) manifest in popular culture at a time when traditional gender dynamics are under particular threat from second wave feminist demands for sexual equality.

To conclude, in order to fully appreciate *The Stepford Wives*, it needs be contextualized within longer histories of fictional imaginings about artificial women, from early industrialization through to sci-fi imaginings of the 1970s. Fantasies about artificial people have existed since antiquity, but tales conflating fears of technological advancement with anxieties about women, and the idea of the feminine, find origin in scientific logic and rationality of the 1800s. Since that time, clear patterns of representation can be identified involving patriarchal endeavors to reduce female sexuality to its most controllable form – as the product of male intervention and invention. As this chapter has shown, the majority of texts leading up to (and including) the 1970s enact this fantasy, of which, *L'Eve Future* is the most histrionic in its contemptuous deconstruction of the feminine, and subsequent reconstruction of an idealized, subservient facsimile. In the subsequent chapters of this book, these themes will be further expanded in the context of second-wave feminism, backlash theory, postfeminism, and lastly, in Chapter 7, in relation to contemporary gender politics, social robotics and AI technologies. However, before discussing the broader political, social, and cultural contexts of *The Stepford Wives*, it is necessary to discuss the environment in which the film was made, particularly in relation to the US film industry at the time, and in regard to the internal politics involved in the production of the film itself.

Chapter 3: *The Stepford Wives* in Hollywood

> *Stepford Wives* was one of the things where a lot of people had a finger in the pie, and I think while the screenplay was good to begin with, I think it sort of got a bit tangled up as things went along and I'm really not crazy about the movie. (Levin in conversation with Sandler, 1992, p.9)

Levin was not the only person who was 'not crazy' about *The Stepford Wives*. Indeed, while the film did relatively well at the box-office to begin with, mainly thanks simultaneous release and 'event' promotion practices employed by major studios at the time, its popularity was not sustained. As William Goldman comments in his book *Adventures of the Screen Trade*, the studios made a good return initially, but it was 'gone in a month' (1984, p.54). Critical responses were mixed; the quality of performances, especially those of Katherine Ross and Paula Prentice, were generally praised, but the film's running time and stylistic choices, including costuming and cinematography, were less well received. Furthermore, as Levin suggests, there were internal tensions on the set, particularly regarding the screenplay, which was originally authored by William Goldman, but changed quite considerably by Forbes. To begin, this chapter will establish the climate of the US film industry in the 1970s before examining the production and behind the scenes conflicts involved in the making of *The Stepford Wives*. The chapter will explore audience and critical responses more broadly; however, feminist reactions and the film's allegiance to the political imperatives of liberal feminism are the focus of Chapter 4.

The US Film Industry in the 1970s

In the early to mid-1970s, Hollywood underwent a major transformation initiated by a film industry repression that began in 1969 and lasted until the end of 1971: a downturn that was, according to David Cook, 'a state of dislocation matched only by the coming of sound' (2000, p.9). Dynamics surrounding the production and reception of *The Stepford Wives* are very much embedded in the socio-cultural climate of this transformative period of Hollywood film history. Therefore, in advance of discussing the making *The Stepford Wives*, it is important to provide some context regarding the US film industry at this time. Writing for *Variety* (1972), A. D. Murphy describes how, by the end of 1968, there was an all-time peak in feature film investment of about $US 1,200,000,000. Yet by 1971, this had been slashed by forty-two percent and losses totalled somewhere in the vicinity of $US 600 million. As Murphy (1972, p.3) maintains, the primary cause of the 1969-1971 Hollywood depression was an over-production boom that took place from 1966 to 1968. In particular, a glut of lavish and exorbitantly expensive musicals was made without sensible consideration for likely return on investment. Hoping to cash in on the success of George Cukor's *My Fair Lady* (1964) and Robert Wise's *The Sound of Music* (1965), musicals such as *Chitty Chitty Bang Bang* (Ken Hughes, 1968) and *Doctor Dolittle* (Richard Fleischer, 1969) were over-invested in by the major film studios, triggering the industry's collapse under the financial burden of record-high costs of borrowing money (Murphy, 1972, p.3; Cook, 2002, p.9).

By the end of 1969, the Hollywood depression had shifted into high gear. Problematic practices at the time included fiscal juggling, where the profits of one film were used to offset losses elsewhere. According to Murphy (1972, p.20), these dealings initiated some major tax changes including the introduction of tax credits for corporate losses and a seven percent tax credit on investment in domestic film production that also allowed profits earned from exports to be deferred and reinvested in local film making. Additionally, it was becoming increasingly expensive to produce films, so significantly fewer were being made by the early 1970s. The average cost of making a film rose some four-hundred-and-fifty percent between 1972 and 1979 and because only a few releases in a given year captured the majority of the box-office dollars, it became evident that fewer films could sustain any major company: The guiding principle was that seven out of ten films will lose money, two out of ten will break even, and one will be an enormous success (See Cook, 2002, p.12; Friedman, 2007, p.4).

Following this logic, only films that were carefully packaged and laden with 'proven' elements had any reasonable chance of becoming blockbusters. Journalist William Paul (1977, p.62) contends that more than ever, Hollywood was on the lookout for 'pre-sold' projects that came with a formula for guaranteed success: 'films based on runaway best-sellers and hit plays, or films with stars who in themselves are so big that they generate their own publicity' (Paul, 1977, p.62). The motion picture industry also embarked on new production approaches of strategic (or scientific) marketing, which involved synchronising the making of a film with its promotion. Francis Ford Coppola's *The Godfather* (1972) was the first film to benefit from this tactic. By the time *The Godfather* was released, it had attained 'event' status through mass sales of Mario Puzo's 1969 novel and intense publicity focused on both the shooting of the film and protests by Italian-American groups about its supposedly prejudiced content. As Cook (2002, p.14) argues, *The Godfather* was such an enormous success at the box office, it almost singlehandedly restored industry confidence.

However, it was the November 1975 release of Steven Spielberg's *Jaws* (adapted from the 1974 novel of the same name by Peter Benchley), and the adoption of saturation booking strategies for big budget blockbusters, that really transformed the industry (Cook, 2002, p.26). Saturation booking – a strategy that involves simultaneous openings in as many theatres as possible – was once reserved for exploitation films where it was used to generate quick profits before negative reviews could get around. Hollywood productions were instead typically released gradually under a model known as 'platform distribution' (Cook, 2002, p.15). But this strategy was no longer effective by the 1970s – instead, it became apparent that going to the cinema had to be presented as a unique experience. Under new corporate management, major film studios created artificial demand by releasing far fewer films (forty percent fewer in 1975 compared to 1970), which were subject to television advertising blitzes. This distribution strategy grew even more effective with the proliferation of Hollywood-sponsored multiplexes. The multiplex dramatically increased the number of screens available for saturation release, while at the same time, the smaller multiplex screens and limited seating further generated a sense of exigency for movie goers.

Because the cost of film making had become so inflated, another strategy employed by major studios was to let independent companies assume the inherent risks of producing films. Hence, according to Lee Beaupre (1972, p.5) it was a common practice in the early 1970s for major studios to buy and distribute films made by independents rather than investing in production themselves. In fact, majors derived one third of their release schedules from independent picture companies at the time. The downside of this practice was that independent films were not promoted as heavily as the major studios own productions with their larger equity investments. Nonetheless, this initially seemed like an exciting opportunity for independent film makers, particularly in the context of vertical integration practices that historically monopolised the industry until the late 1940s. Cook (2002, p.19) maintains that to begin, independent producers benefited very well from the blockbuster-driven product shortage, quickly filling the gap created by the major studios in their partial abandonment of the field. Independent films accounted for about two-thirds of all American production at the time. However, they only generated ten-to-fifteen percent of the box office and rental market. Therefore, despite the investments in indie film making, the reality was that without connections to a major distributor, the chances of recuperating costs was poor. As Lawrence Cohen explains (1980, p.13), without a tie to a major distributor, an indie film stood only a fifty percent chance of getting a domestic theatrical release in the US; hence, by the end of the 1970s, only a few producers enjoyed the continuous patronage of a major studio. The rest spent a great deal of time looking for development capital and existing from deal-to-deal.

Making *The Stepford Wives*

The Stepford Wives had all the right ingredients for success. The original novel, though not as celebrated as Levin's earlier masterpiece *Rosemary's Baby*, was nonetheless a bestseller and the film adaptation held strong promise, particularly considering the outstanding triumph of Polanski's cinematic version of *Rosemary's Baby*. After all, the elemental plot structure of the two narratives have much in common: both are gothic women's stories, both involve an initial impression of normalcy, followed by a wife's belief that her husband is conspiring against her, followed by gradual descent into a waking nightmare.

Novelist and screenwriter William Goldman is formally credited with the screenplay, which was acquired by the independent production company Palomar Pictures International. Goldman had an established reputation having previously written the original screenplay *Butch Cassidy and the Sundance Kid* (George Hill, 1969). He would later go on to write the screenplay for *All the President's Men* (Alan J. Pakula, 1976) and both the novel and screenplay for *The Princess Bride* (Rob Reiner, 1987). However, in Appendix One of Forbes' memoir *A Divided Life* (1992) he includes *The Stepford Wives* as part of his screenwriting career, listing himself as having written the 'full screenplay, no credit' (1992, p.358) – the rationale being that he significantly developed Goldman's work and wrote the final shooting script himself, something Goldman also concedes, claiming that Forbes almost completely re-created *The Stepford Wives*, save for the ending: 'The last quarter of the movie is mine. I think he [Forbes] would have changed that too, but he ran out of time' (Goldman, 1981, p.154).

Palomar was founded by prominent producer Edgar J. Scherick, who is well known for pioneering network sports broadcasting and the creation of the series *Wide World of Sports* (1961-1998) through his company Sports Programming. Scherick later sold Sports Programming to the American Broadcasting Company (ABC) and eventually became vice president for programming on ABC's television network where he created popular shows such as *Bewitched* (1964-1972), *Batman* (1966-1968), and *That Girl* (1966-1971). Following the completion of the production phase of *The Stepford Wives* with Palomar, it was contracted to Columbia Pictures, which secured ownership for theatrical releases and promoted the movie as a much anticipated event – a practice that had become standard by at time. As soon as filming on location began, hype was generated via media reportage. A *Boxoffice* article (June 17 1974) describes the ten-week shooting schedule for the film 'based on Levin's chilling new bestselling novel' (1974, p.105); the shooting locations (including NYC, Westport, Redding Ridge, Fairfield, and Weston); and the excitement of local residents, many of whom were employed as extras and whose private homes were used as sets.[9] Promotional posters were simple yet provocative, asking questions such as: 'Where do all the men go at night in the town of Stepford?' 'Why is the town of Stepford a nice place to visit…but not to live?' and 'Are there really men who would move their wives to Stepford?' Following the film's February release, it is reported that some theatres ran publicity campaigns to stimulate ticket sales. Another *Boxoffice* article (June 23 1975) describes how the managers of a cinema in Jackson, Florida organised competitions for free tickets with a local radio station. In anticipation that the film would appeal mainly to women, the same theatre also offered events where women would be admitted for one dollar if they drove to the cinema in a station wagon, or presented a photo of them driving one (station wagons being the preferred utilitarian car for 'busy Stepford housewives').

Although the actual shooting of the film went smoothly, it is well documented that there were tensions behind the scenes, particularly between Goldman and Forbes. Scherick originally gave Goldman's script to Brian De Palma because he liked De Palma's psychological thriller *Sisters* (1972). According to Scherick, De Palma loved the script, but when Scherick informed Goldman, Goldman asserted that if De Palma was hired, he would want nothing to do with the picture again (it is not clear why). Hence, Scherick offered the role of director to Forbes. Scherick's rationale was that the film 'needed some intelligence behind it' (Gregory, 2001). He also thought that an English director would offer an interesting external perspective on American suburban life (Monahan, 2004). By 1974, Forbes had an established reputation for excellence following films such as *Whistle Down the Wind* (1961), *The L-Shaped Room* (1962), *Séance on a Wet Afternoon* (1964) and *The Whisperers* (1967), and although he had no knowledge of Levin's book beforehand he was enthusiastic about the project (Monahan, 2004).

An initial point of conflict between Forbes and Goldman occurred when Forbes decided to redraft the script. Forbes thought that the screenplay was good, but in need of development – Scherick also agreed that Goldman's screenplay could be improved, and so Forbes reworked it, adding in a lot of 'sacred and profane aspects of himself' (Gregory, 2001) and reportedly changing the ending significantly before shooting commenced, although this sits in direct opposition to Goldman's claims that the ending remained his. In an interview with Mark Monahan for *The Telegraph* (2004), Forbes expresses that he was not happy with the fact that he received no official credit as a screenwriter, explaining that: 'I didn't get on with Goldman. Whenever I needed him he was either in analysis or at basketball games. He didn't like English directors – or maybe he didn't like directors. But I thought his screenplay lacked certain elements that I wanted to get in' (Monahan 2004).

Forbes' supposition that Goldman disliked directors is supported by Goldman's

The Stepford Wives

comments to journalist Alex Ward in an interview for *American Film* (1976). According to Ward, Goldman emphatically states that he is not a screenwriter, but a novelist who also writes screenplays. For Goldman, screenwriting is demeaning 'shit work' that is 'denigrating to the soul' (Ward, 1976, p.30). Ward suggests that part of Goldman's distain for screenwriting has to do with the creative processes of moviemaking for writers who do not direct their own material: 'what the screenwriter writes isn't necessarily what gets filmed. Changes are made, egos get bruised, tempers fray, and bad feelings result' (Ward, 1976, p.30). Goldman's view is that the screenwriter does all the preliminary hard work trying to get an idea down on paper, then the director takes over, carrying it across the finishing line – receiving the bulk of the credit. Accordingly, Goldman sees directors as over-praised and natural adversaries of screenwriters. As Ward states, one of Goldman's most displeasing experiences of his career was with *The Stepford Wives*, due to the disagreements he had with Forbes. Goldman claims that the finished film was so different from his screenplay, he would not have agreed to the project in the first place had he known what the result would be (Ward, 1976, p.30).

The decision to cast Nanette Newman (Forbes' muse and wife) as Carol Van Sant caused even greater fiction between Goldman and Forbes. In fact, Goldman blamed the entire US box-office failure of the film on the casting of Newman in what was a relatively minor role – something that Forbes was outraged about and deeply offended by. Goldman describes how he realised the project was doomed when early on, before shooting, Forbes commented that he thought Nanette would be good for the part of Carol. Goldman envisaged the replica wives to look like voluptuous playmates, costumed in summer shorts, T-shirts, and tennis whites. However, for Goldman, Newman was too old and definitely not a sex bomb. Citing Goldman:

> If you are [...] so obsessed with women being nothing but subordinate sex objects, if you are willing to spend the rest of your days humping a piece of plastic – well, shit, that plastic better goddam well be in the form of Bo Derek. You don't commit murder and make a new creation to have it look like Nanette Newman. Not only that, but having Nanette Newman in the part, the whole look of the film had to alter. Forget the tennis costumes. Forget the parade of Bunnies walking through the A&P in shorts on their perfect tanned legs. She can't wear the clothes.

> Which is why [...] all these women in the summertime in Stepford, Connecticut, walk around in long dresses to the floor and big brimmed hats on their heads. (Goldman, 1981, pp.155-6)[10]

In Levin's novel, Carol Van Sant is described as a tall, leggy, red-head with 'big bobbing breasts' (1972, pp.9-10) – a description that fits with what Goldman had in mind. Nonetheless, the claim that Forbes chose to costume the wives anachronistically based entirely on the fact that Newman did not adhere to a *Playboy* Bunny aesthetic is unfounded. In David Gregory's documentary about the film, Paula Prentice claims that the costuming choices were intended to speak back to pervasively outmoded notions about women – ideas that belong in the Victorian era. The mechanical wives, including Carol, are shot in soft focus, further emphasising fanciful nostalgia for an era before feminism, when married women were compelled to be subservient to the wants of their husbands. This sits in stark contrast to how Joanna and Bobby (Paula Prentice) are presented: filmed in standard focus and outfitted in minimalist tops with no bra, bare midriffs and hip-hugging flared jeans – the attire of independent, politically conscious 1970s women who are comfortable with their bodies and their sexuality.

Presenting the 'replaced' wives of Stepford as Bunnies and sex bombs may well have underscored the satirical overtones of the narrative, providing more humour, which critic Roger Ebert suggested the film was lacking (1975). Except, it would also have stripped *The Stepford Wives* of the psychological horror and 'creepiness' that makes it so compelling, lessening the pungent commentary about the insidiousness of patriarchal power that contributes to the film's cultural significance and cult status today. Despite personal differences, what Forbes and Goldman had in mind (in keeping with Levin's intents), was for *The Stepford Wives* to be a feminist film: Goldman even interviewed Betty Friedan and other prominent feminists at the time. While Ebert and other commentators are critical of the film's gothic style, ominous overtones, and black humour, without these, the feminist message may well have been muted and trivialised. As established in Chapter 1, much of Levin's work is situated in the tradition of the female gothic, an established genre primarily concerned with women's experiences in a patriarchal world. By filming *The Stepford Wives* in the tone of this style, Forbes successfully conveys the intention of *The*

Figure 4: Costuming the Stepford wives

Stepford Wives as allegory for the political and ideological concerns of second wave feminism. Forbes' aesthetic choices, including his decision to shoot exteriors as light saturated and over exposed, contrasting with cold shadowy interiors emphasising the menace and artificiality of Stepford and its inhabitants, add further gravitas to the film's female gothic sensibilities.

There were other points of contention regarding the making of the film. As detailed in *The Stepford Life*, Goldman's ideal casting choice for Joanna was either Mary Tyler More or Valarie Harper. However, Scherick, after much indecision, finally settled on Diane Keaton (though this did not work out either). As Forbes recalls:

> Casting does not always go smoothly. I remember that during the preparations for *The Stepford Wives*, which I shot in New York and Connecticut, I had a producer who constantly came up with new ideas for the leading lady. It would be discourteous of me to list the many famous names who were first considered and then, for one reason or another, discarded. I spent many frustrating weeks getting nowhere until he decided that his choice would be Diane Keaton. This was fine by me, I admire her extravagantly and looked forward to working with her. We duly met and spent a pleasant afternoon together going over the script. When we said goodbye I fondly imagined that our quest was finally over. However, the following morning she rang me and said that, sadly, she had changed her mind. 'What happened between last night and this morning?' I asked. 'My analyst read the script and got very bad vibes from it,' she said. That was the first and only time I have been rejected by an analyst. (Forbes, 1992, p.27)

While Katherine Ross may not have been the first choice for the lead role, her performance, along with that of Paula Prentice (also not a first option – Joanna Cassidy was originally hired for the role of Bobby, but Scherick fired her after deciding that she was not right for the part after all), was typically praised by film critics and reviewers. One prominent exception is a review by Pauline Kael for *The New Yorker* (1975, pp.110-13), which is scathing of the film in general, commenting that the characters (including Ross) are robotic even before they are turned into robots, that the dialogue is gummy, and the script is patchwork. Molly Haskell, writing for *The Village Voice* (1975, p.66) comments that *The Stepford Wives* does not appeal to primal emotions like *Rosemary's Baby* does, nor does it have the 'incomparable advantage of Roman Polanski's direction,' which Haskell describes as 'straightforward.' For Haskell (1975, p.66), Forbes over directs, is portentous, and invests scenes with overtones of terror that are never explained.

The film was also criticised for its long running-time and slow building tension. For instance, *Variety* describes *The Stepford Wives* as a 'quietly freaky suspense-horror story that takes maddeningly long to evolve.' The review's author goes on to assert that the 'black humour and sophistication of the plot is handled extremely well and never gets out of hand, but at 114 minutes (the first hour is much too overdone) there is a problem of sustaining audience interest. But the last 45 minutes move very well' (*Variety* Feb 12, 1975). Similarly, a review in *The Independent Film Journal* (Feb 19,1975, p.75) criticises the film for being 'little more than science fiction coupled with an ironic parable on the fruits of male chauvinism that has virtually no atmosphere of horror and is too leisurely paced to be justified' (1975, p.75).

There is some merit in comments regarding the film's pace, which certainly is measured. The film takes its time in carefully aligning audiences with Joanna's subjectivity and gradually creates tension in a way that underscores exactly how diabolical the male characters are. As discussed in Chapter 1, elusive sensations of foreboding are fundamental to gothic horror. Through restrained but telling visual motifs, cinematography, and sound score a sense of *unheimlich* is achieved with powerful effect. This mode of psychological horror was not new in 1975, but it was a style that was more popular in the 1960s, primarily due to the success of Hitchcock's *Psycho* (1960) and *Rosemary's Baby*, as well as other psychological thrillers like

Robert Aldrich's *Whatever Happened to Baby Jane?* (1962) and *Hush-Hush Sweet Charlotte* (1964). By the 1970s, popular horror was more bloody and inclined towards high tension. *Let's Scare Jessica to Death* (John D. Hancock, 1971), *Silent Night, Bloody Night* (Theodore Gershuny, 1972), *The Texas Chainsaw Massacre* (Tobe Hooper, 1974), and *Black Christmas* (Bob Clark, 1974) are just some examples of films circulating at this time. It is likely that (younger) audiences had come to expect horror to be more in keeping with this slasher style. It is also possible that audiences had become used to tighter, faster paced, harder hitting releases in general. While *The Stepford Wives* does feel like a long film, the running time (at 115 minutes) is less than *Rosemary's Baby* (at 137 minutes) and other slowly evolving sci-fi films like *2001: A Space Odyssey* (149 minutes). However, in comparison to sci-fi films like *THX 1138* (86 minutes), *Silent Running* (89 minutes), and *Westworld* (88 minutes), which were all released just prior to *The Stepford Wives*, the film is considerably longer.

Overall, despite Columbia's strategies of bulk booking and event release, *The Stepford Wives* did not perform well in the box office. According to Goldman (1981, p. 20), the studio did make money from the film initially, due to its release in hundreds of cinemas nationally, but this did not last. Ratings published in *Boxoffice magazine* (3 March – 31 March 1975) show that *The Stepford Wives* began with strong sales in the first two weeks, but this rapidly dropped off, unlike other films such as *Earthquake* (Mark Robson, 1974), *The Godfather II* (Frances Ford Coppola, 1974), and *Young Frankenstein* (Mel Brooks, 1974) which were still screening in theatres at the same time. Indeed, the film's poor returns meant that *The Stepford Wives* was not made available in the UK until 1978 – the same year that Forbes' family drama *International Velvet* was released. *The Stepford Wives* initially screened at the London Film Festival in 1976. Then, in the absence of a UK distribution deal, it was picked up by the new manager of London's Essential Cinema Club, Derek Hill. According to a *Variety* article (29 December, 1976), Hill had been developing his Soho cinema club as a place to screen arthouse films eschewed by other distributors. The idea was that by showing *The Stepford Wives* at Essential Cinema, enough press and public interest might be generated to warrant wider release (1976, p.30). This strategy worked and the film gradually built the cult status it has today. However, the film was met with scathing criticism from liberal feminists, in particular Betty Friedan, despite the fact that *The Stepford Wives* was openly intended as a creative account of her manifesto *The Feminine Mystique*. This will be examined next.

Chapter 4: *The Stepford Wives* and Liberal Feminism

> Q: 'I read somewhere that some of the feminists were not happy with *Stepford Wives* and that surprised me in a way because I would think that you actually characterised that life that many feminists complain of.'
>
> A: 'Yes, I intended it to be sympathetic to feminists and I felt it was, and I think as the years have passed I don't hear objections any more. You know, feminists now will say that they like the book and they see it as being on the women's side.'
>
> (Levin in conversation with Sandler, 1992, p.9)

Despite Levin's intention for *The Stepford Wives* to be read as pro-feminist, both the book and the film received polarising reactions in relation to the sexual politics of the narrative. From a contemporary perspective, *The Stepford Wives* clearly speaks back to some of the most salient concerns of liberal feminism of the 1960s and early 1970s, specifically the problems faced by white, middle-class, suburban housewives – the focus of Betty Friedan's *The Feminine Mystique*. The robot wives of Stepford operate as allegory for 'the feminine mystique' – an ideological myth about self-fulfilment that women were inculcated to aspire to following World War II. As Friedan asserts:

> They [women] were taught to pity the neurotic, unfeminine, unhappy women who wanted to be poets or physicians or presidents. They learned that truly feminine women did not want careers, higher education, political rights – the independence and the opportunities that the old-fashioned feminists fought for [...]. A thousand expert voices applauded their femininity, their adjustment, their new maturity. All they had to do was devote their lives from earliest girlhood to finding a husband and bearing children. (Friedan, 1963, p.16)

The subjective horrors experienced by Joanna as she confronts the tacit realities and expectations of being a suburban housewife, of embodying the 'cherished' mystique of feminine fulfilment, articulate what Friedan refers to as 'the problem that has no name' – a desperate, empty feeling often felt by housewives, but not discussed: a silent crisis causing middle-class women to question what kind of wives/mothers they were if they did not feel an enigmatic sense of fulfilment waxing the kitchen floor and ironing their husband's shirts, leading them to unspoken conclusions that there must be something was wrong with their marriages, themselves, that they were hopelessly neurotic, or completely losing their minds (Friedan, 1963, p.19). As Pat Mainari states in her well-known paper 'The Politics of Housework': 'We women have been brainwashed more than we can ever imagine. Probably too many years of seeing television women in ecstasy over shiny waxed floors or breaking down over their dirty shirt collars' (1969).

Levin makes explicit reference to Friedan, writing her into a scene where Joanna discovers an old newspaper article detailing the existence of a Stepford Women's Club and a scheduled talk given by Friedan to its fifty-plus members (Levin, 1972, p.42). Additionally, he includes a quote from Simone de Beauvoir's formative *The Second Sex* (1949) in the epitaph of *The Stepford Wives*, further underscoring the novel's allegiance to feminist liberation. Likewise, the film is faithful to Levin's original narrative and clearly shares the same loyalty to feminist causes, despite its pessimistic ending. Indeed, as mentioned in Chapter 3, Goldman went so far as to interview Friedan and other prominent women's rights activists at the time in order to ensure feminist credentials. It is surprising then, that some activists, including Friedan herself, were outraged by the cinematic release of *The Stepford Wives* – particularly given the film's obvious debt to Friedan's work. Many critics were similarly rejecting of the film's feminist sensibilities. This chapter will explore these reactions in the context of the popular media climate at the time and in relation to prominent feminist publications, particularly Friedan's work. This chapter also offers an extended discussion about the limits of Friedan's writing, particularly in the context of subsequent critiques by theorists, including bell hooks. The purpose of this is not to undermine the feminist intentions of *The Stepford Wives*, but rather to acknowledge some glaring limitations of Friedan's work from a contemporary perspective.

Feminist Diatribe or 'Rip-Off'?

Following the cinematic release of *The Stepford Wives*, responses from feminist activists were highly polarising, tending towards either exuberant praise or scathing rejection. Chapter 3 examined broader reactions from critics in relation to aspects including the film's running time, pace, casting, and aesthetic choices. However, by far the liveliest commentary related to the production's veracity as a feminist text. This included unexpected and scathing criticism from Betty Friedan herself. In response to mixed critical reviews, and in an attempt to generate more box-office sales, Columbia Pictures organised a special screening of *The Stepford Wives* in New York, followed by an 'awareness session' involving one hundred women 'opinion makers.' This was hosted by Eleanor Perry, one of the film industry's more vocal feminists at the time and screenwriter for *Diary of a Mad Housewife* (Frank Perry, 1970). The idea was for women to discuss their views about the film's politics (Helford, 2003, p.24). According to Judy Klemesrud (1975), a number of awareness session attendees were completely outraged by the film, including Friedan, who declared it a 'rip-off of the women's movement' before storming out after only 10 minutes. Other attendees described it as 'completely ridiculous' and 'junk that should not be taken seriously.' Some complained about the fact that it was made by men, arguing that 'women should write and direct their own movies if they are ever to have any intelligent "women's pictures".' Writer Linda Arking commented that the film 'confirms every fear we ever had about the battle of the sexes and it says there is no way for people to get together and lead human lives' (Klemesrud, 1975, p.29; Helford, 2003, p.24).

Reproaches emerging from the awareness session echo negative critical responses more broadly. Herbert Gans argues that *The Stepford Wives* paints an 'uncomplimentary picture of feminism and women. The men see women's lib as a terrible threat, but for the women it is mainly an antidote to suburban boredom and unhappy marriage, with the economic and political demands made by the women's movement left out' (1975, p.60). Echoing Arking's remarks, Gans further asserts that by pitting women against men, *The Stepford Wives* ignores feminists who argue that women's liberation cannot be achieved without larger social change that also liberates men. He proposes that the film is little more than an expression of Levin, Goldman, and Forbes' own fears about women and women's liberation (Gans, 1975, p.60). The claim that *The Stepford Wives* sets women against men as rivals is echoed by other critics too. Kael claims that the film says to men 'you're a vacuous, inadequate excuse for a man; you've been demeaning a sensitive, intelligent woman, and now that she's trying to lift her head and get her consciousness raised, you'd rather kill her than let her find herself' (Kael, 1975, p.112). Similarly, Richard Schickel (1975, p.3) asserts: 'Obviously, *The Stepford Wives* aspires to be a women's lib parable, realising the female's worst fears about her mate's desire to dehumanize her. But it is so glibly on the side of the fashionable angels. Moreover, the movie never shows a single man whose ideal exceeds gatefold dimensions. That too is a form of dehumanization' (1975, p.3). Anya Krugovoy Silver proposes that this may have been one of the reasons for Friedan's vehement rejection of the film – that it fails to offer a vision of men and women working together for the betterment of their lives as a whole, rather 'it envisions men who are willing to kill in order to preserve their male prerogative' (Krugovoy Silver, 2002, pp.62-3). It must be noted that Friedan did not actually specify why she hated *The Stepford Wives*. However, as Joanne Boucher points out, Friedan was adamant that the women's movement present itself as 'reasonable, moderate, heterosexual, family-loving not family destroying, man-loving not man-hating in its approach' (Friedan, 1963, p.3; Boucher, 2003, p.23).

Haskell describes the Stepford wife as a product of puritanical woman's ideals: 'a punitive figure spirited by women rather than a wish-fulfilment fantasy for the pleasure of men' (1975, p.66) based on the fact that, in Haskell's opinion, it is women who compulsively obsess over housekeeping, not their husbands. Haskell concludes that 'beneath all the women's lib paraphernalia, this is just one more sermon on the mind numbing effects of suburbia and television' (1975, p.66). Kael defines the film as condescending and degrading in its implicit view that educated American women are not responsible for what they become (1975, pp.110-13). According to Kael, if women turn into replicas of commercials they do it to themselves. Kael further claims that by blaming the barrenness of their lives on men, the women of Stepford play at being victims under the guise of liberation, essentially rendering the film a 'women's lib continuation of a soap opera' providing nothing but 'drab masochism' (1975, p.112).

However, feminist and critical reactions were not universally negative. Klemesrud explains that the awareness session attendees also praised the film for its relatability, particularly to the fact that a lot of men 'really do want wives who are robots.'

The Stepford Wives

Eleanor Perry is reported to have stated: 'Finally, a movie that is not about two guys and their adventures [...] The film presses buttons that make you furious – the fact that all the Stepford men wanted were big breasts, big bottoms, a clean house, fresh-perked coffee and sex. I thought for sure Betty Friedan would stand up and say, "Yes, this is just the way men treat women"' (Klemesrud, 1975, p.29). Perry's point is an important one. *The Stepford Wives* consciously critiques patriarchal attitudes and assumptions in a way that is intended to make pro-feminist viewers furious – from more subtle behaviours such as Walter's failure to include Joanna in any actual decision making (it's always about him and what he wants), to the most extreme forms of representation availed through the use of sci-fi and horror conventions. Writing for *Cinefantastique* (1975), David Bartholomew asserts that *The Stepford Wives* 'uses extremes to effective purpose because the genre, in this case a mixture of horror and science fiction/fantasy, will support it by definition. The film can discuss reality without having to attempt it' (1975, p.40). Bartholomew also makes the claim that *The Stepford Wives* is 'one of the select few genre films more important for its ideas than its genre excitements':

> Forbes and Goldman have done an astonishing thing with their theme (and Levin's fast-read novel) – they have casually turned it into a vastly successful metaphor for the plight of women and their movement for liberation and then use that specific, rightfully, as a plea for human freedom as a whole. *The Stepford Wives* is probably the only valuable, intellectually conceived movie about women and their future made in the past decade. (Bartholomew, 1975, p.40)

As Krugovoy Silver (2002, pp.60-3) rightly argues, the themes of *The Stepford Wives* dovetail so closely with those of second-wave feminism that it ultimately owes too much to feminist theories to be dismissed as merely a parody of them, like some critics suggest. The Stepford husbands are symbolic of the way hegemony operates more broadly. The men silently work behind the scenes to maintain sexual inequality and the subordination of women in the same way that organisations operate to maintain power hierarchies on social, political, and economic levels. The husbands' misogynistic pact to reinstate their women as visually enhanced, psychically one-dimensional, leak free, versions of 1950s housewives is indicative of real world political agendas following World War II. As Friedan maintains, in the fifteen years following the war, the mystique of feminine fulfilment became the cherished and self-perpetuating core of American culture:

> Millions of women lived their lives in the image of those pretty pictures of the American suburban housewife, kissing their husbands goodbye in front of the picture window, depositing their stationwagonsful of children at school, and smiling as they ran the new electric waxer over the spotless kitchen floor [...]. Their only dream was to be perfect wives and mothers, their highest ambition to have five children and a beautiful house, their only fight to get and keep their husbands. They had no thought for the unfeminine problems of the world outside the home; they wanted the men to make the major decisions. They glorified in their role as women, and wrote proudly on the census blank: "Occupation: Housewife." (Friedan, 1963, p.18)

One reason why reactions to the politics of *The Stepford Wives* were so vehemently critiqued has to do with broader relationships between second-wave feminism and 1970s mainstream media, which was often problematic. According to Elyse Helford, popular media at this time trivialised feminist conscious-raising mantras like 'The Personal is Political' and 'Sisterhood is Powerful,' ridiculed women's public demonstrations, and demonised feminists as abrasive, unattractive troublemakers. At the same time popular media capitalized on calls to sisterhood by pitting men against women through the use of antagonistic or warlike rhetoric such as 'battle of the sexes.' The primary goal of these so called 'battles' was to show who was better, smarter, more equipped to handle power, and more worthy of respect (Helford, 2003, pp.25-9). A prominent example is the 1973 tennis face-offs between Bobby Riggs and Margaret Court in a $10,000 USD winner-takes-all challenge and later another 'battle of the sexes' challenge between Bobby Riggs and Billie Jean King, which King won. Television series like *Bewitched* and *I Dream of Jeannie* (Sidney Sheldon, 1965-1970) made light of political conscious raising through depictions of intelligent women who choose not to wield their power, instead preferring to remain in the domestic sphere and subservient to their conspicuously ordinary mortal husbands (Helford, 2003, p.26). Women's liberation was further undermined in shows such as *Charlie's Angels* (ABC, 1976-1981) which depicts the three central female characters as active, savvy, police academy-trained private detectives, but at the same time hyper-sexualises them and, as the title of the show suggests, locates them squarely under the control of an invisible patriarch called Charlie.[11]

CBS's *My Living Doll* (1964-1965) focuses on a robot prototype named Rhonda or AF709 (Julie Newmar) who ends up in the possession of an Air Force psychiatrist called Bob McDonald (played by Bob Cummings). McDonald takes Rhonda home and proceeds to teach her how to be a perfect domesticated woman – one that 'does what she's told' and 'doesn't talk back.' A precursor to *My Living Doll* is Lester Del Rey's short sci-fi story 'Helen O'Loy' (1938). 'Helen O'Loy' is about two men (Dave and Phill) who cannot get along with real women, so they buy a 'girl-modelled' utility robot. After some home modifications that include electrical rewiring and chemically based emotional enhancement, they set her to work as a domestic servant. However, stuck at home all day, Helen becomes addicted to television love stories and soap operas – the perfect outlet for her newly heightened 'feelings.' With little else to think about, she falls in love with Dave and transforms into a hyper attentive, clingy, needy, desperate housewife, driving Dave to despair and alcoholism. With misogynist texts like this as a forerunner, coupled with the media atmosphere more broadly at the time, it is unsurprising that some feminists and critics assumed *The Stepford Wives* was attacking second-wave feminism. Taken at face value, factors including authorship – the film was written, scripted, and directed by privileged white, heterosexual men, the husbands of Stepford clearly have more social, economic, and political power than the women, and, importantly, the wives fatefully lose in their 'battle of the sexes' against their husbands – work to reinforce this perspective on *The Stepford Wives*. However, as previously discussed, this view fails to take into account the film's complex engagement with some of the most salient concerns of the women's liberation movement of the 1960s and 1970s. Forbes' dystopic vision of suburban America is not only in keeping with traditions of the gothic women's film discussed in Chapter One, including a focus on the heroine's subjective experiences, but as Krugovoy Silver (2002, p.63) suggests, it is much too faithful to the manifestos of prominent activists at the time to be written off as yet another media attack on feminism.

Limits of *The Feminine Mystique*

Before examining how *The Stepford Wives* operates as a creative articulation of *The Feminine Mystique* and 'the problem with no name', it is important to draw attention to some major limitations of Friedan's feminist politics. This in turn provides a fuller understanding of some of the visual and thematic choices in the film. Friedan's work, and the kind of liberal feminism it endorses, has unequivocally been instrumental to women's rights. As Daniel Horowitz points out, Friedan's book was a key factor in the revival of the women's movement and in generating awareness to the challenges faced by white, middle-class, heterosexual, suburban women (1998, p.197). But Friedan's brand of activism, with its singular focus on this narrow group as victims of sexual discrimination, has attracted considerable critique, and rightly so. Ignored are those marginalised by race, class, poverty, (dis)ability, sexuality and a host of other intersecting factors. As bell hooks argues: 'Feminism in the United States has never emerged from the women who are most victimised by sexist oppression; women who are powerless to change their condition in life. They are the silent majority' (2000, p.1). While Friedan's *The Feminist Mystique* is heralded as having paved the way for second wave feminism, it was written as if these women did not exist:

> Friedan's famous phrase, "the problem that has no name," often quoted to describe the condition of women in this society, actually referred to the plight of a select group of college-educated, middle- and upper-class, married white women – housewives bored with leisure, with the home, with the children, with buying products, who wanted more out of life. Friedan concludes her first chapter by stating: "We can no longer ignore that voice within women that says: 'I want something more than my husband and my children and my house.'" That "more" she defined as careers. She did not discuss who would be called in to take care of the children and maintain the home if women like herself were freed from their house labor and given equal access with white men to the professions. She did not speak of the needs of women without men, without children, without homes. She ignored the existence of all non-white women and poor white women. She did not tell readers whether it was more fulfilling to be a maid, a babysitter, a factory worker, a clerk, or a prostitute than to be a leisure-class housewife. (hooks, 2000, pp.1-2)

According to hooks, not only did Friedan and other liberal feminists have little knowledge of, or concern for, the problems of lower class and poor women, or the particular problems of non-white women from all classes, they were also unwilling to change the movement's focus so that it would better address the needs of women on the whole (hooks, 2014, p.188). Instead, the plight of white, middle-class, heterosexual women were made synonymous with problems afflicting all American women and sexism was treated as the ultimate oppression. Due to these universalising practices, second wave feminism is sometimes referred to as 'hegemonic feminism' (Sandoval, 2000, pp.41-2; Thompson, 2002, p.337).

Friedan's one-dimensional approach to women's rights is reflective of the privileged position from which it comes. However, it seems to move beyond this as well. In a dialogue between Friedan and de Beauvoir published in the *Saturday Review* in 1975, Friedan claims that attempts to make political ideology out of lesbianism 'has diverted energies from the political mainstream and hindered the political momentum of the Women's Movement' (Friedan, p.14). This accusation reveals that Friedan is not just inconsiderate of the issues and concerns of other groups of women, but that she actively opposes them, disclosing a degree of homophobia in the process. However, for hooks, the pinnacle of Friedan's conceit occurs in Chapter Twelve of *The Feminine Mystique*: 'Progressive Dehumanization' (2000, p.3). Here, Friedan compares the impact of domestic confinement and isolation to dehumanizing experiences in Nazi concentration camps: 'the conditions which destroyed the human identity of so many prisoners were not the torture and the brutality, but conditions similar to those which destroy the identity of the American housewife' (Friedan, 1963, pp.305-6). Friedan goes on to validate her comparison by asserting that just like housewives, prisoners in camps were forced to adopt childlike behaviour, give up their individuality, and merge into an amorphous mass – dehumanizing processes that eroded their self-determination and self-respect (1963, p.306). To compare the daily experiences of middle-class housewives to imprisonment at Ravensbrück, Treblinka, Dachau, Auschwitz-Birkenau, or any other of the many concentration (or extermination) camps built by the Nazis is tasteless and ignorant on Friedan's part.

Stepford and the women who live there are clearly intended to reflect the kind of privileged women Friedan focused on for her book: two hundred of her former college classmates from Smith Private Women's Liberal Arts College in Northampton, Massachusetts (Friedan, 1963, p.11). The fictional town of Stepford, set in the neighbouring county of Connecticut, is comfortably upper-middle-class, monochromatically white, and inhabited by once intelligent (likely college educated) women who inevitably fall victim to the feminine mystique. Not until the closing sequence, set in the town's supermarket, is there any visual variant on the bland Anglo-centrism of Stepford. Here, in the midst of the automated wives, leisurely gliding around costumed in floppy hats and maxi-dresses are a hip looking Black couple – the most recent new residents of Stepford. This is very much an acknowledgement of slow shifts occurring in relation to civil rights, a burgeoning Black middle-class, and early smattering of racial diversity in once exclusively white suburban enclaves. According to hooks, in the post-World War II era, '[B]lack and white women alike were subjected to endless propaganda which encouraged them to believe that a woman's place was in the home – that her fulfilment in life depended on finding the right man to marry and produce a family' (hooks, 2014, p.165). Acknowledgement of these dynamics takes *The Stepford Wives* beyond *The Feminine Mystique*, which does not extend past the life experiences of Friedan herself. However, this is not to suggest that the film is more progressive than Friedan's work, rather the passing inclusion of a Black couple denotes some of the social shifts that had taken place over the twelve years since Friedan's writing in 1963.

Another criticism levelled at Friedan is her failure to formally acknowledge the influence of Simone de Beauvoir's *The Second Sex*. de Beauvoir's pivotal work is an intellectual exercise in existential philosophy addressing critical questions regarding what it means to be a woman and the socially constructed organisation of sex differences. Granted, this does make it significantly less accessible to the masses than Friedan's mainstream publication, which offers considerably more superficial critiques and solutions to women's issues. However, it is difficult to overlook the many parallels between the two texts, particularly in relation to housework, motherhood, and marriage. As Sandra Dijkstra argues, at the centre of *The Feminine Mystique* is de Beauvoir's crucial discovery 'One is not born, but rather becomes, woman' (de Beauvoir, 2009, p. 293). However, instead of analysing the phenomenon that there is no biological, physical or economic destiny that defines the role taken on by women in society (de Beauvoir, 2009, p. 293), and rather than examining the specific institutions that oppress women (housework, motherhood, marriage), Friedan limits her attack to more superficial enemies – media, social sciences, and consumerism – 'themselves not the *cause*, but rather the *means*: the agents by which the subordinate condition of women is ideologically maintained and reinforced' (Dijkstra, 1980, p.295). Hence, Friedan's claim that it was a 'personal question mark' (1963, p.11) that first led to her project is misleading. It is not until some twenty-two years after *The Second Sex* was first translated into English in 1953 that Friedan finally admitted to the influence of de Beauvoir's work on her own writing. In a feature appearing in the *Saturday Review* (1975 pp.16-17), Friedan concedes that she learned her own existentialism from de Beauvoir and that:

> It was *The Second Sex* that introduced me to an existential approach to reality and political responsibility [...] To be more precise, when I first read *The Second Sex*, in the early fifties, I was writing 'housewife' on the census blanks, still in the unanalysed embrace of the feminine mystique. And the book's effect on me personally as a woman was depressing [...] Only after a dozen years of living that kind of life did I personally, concretely, analyse what had bought me and other American women to that depressing state. (Freidan, 1975, p.16)

This reads as something of a backhanded and begrudging admission that still clings to Friedan's original claim that it was a *'personal'* question mark that leads her to interviewing women and subsequently the publication of her book. She further accuses de Beauvoir of speaking about women with an authority that seems sterile, cold, and far removed from the real lives of women: 'Somehow, she did not seem to identify with ordinary women, trying to make something new of their own lives or to feel at all involved with their every-day problems' (1975, p.17). This is an interesting claim given that Friedan neglects to identify with most classes of 'ordinary' women in her own work.

Another publication that makes similar observations to Friedan is Stephan Taylor's 1938 paper 'The Suburban Neurosis,' which details, from a clinical perspective, the plight of the British suburban housewife, trapped in a marriage to Mr Everyman – a typically dull individual who has a secure job, but is useless in bed (1938, p.759). Taylor describes the key causes of suburban neurosis as: boredom, created by intense loneliness, lack of friends, not enough to do, and not enough to think about; anxiety about money and the house and accidently getting pregnant (again); and displaced values created by a fetishisation of the home (Taylor, 1938, pp.759-61): 'Physical love is a disappointment, the husband turns out to be rather ordinary and grumpy, the house is seen for what it is, a jerry-built box, and even the child is not as wonderful as was hoped [...] They [housewives] have nothing to look forward to, nothing to look up to, and little to live for' (Taylor, 1938, p.761). It is entirely possible that Friedan was not aware of this publication, but the aetiology introduced by Taylor is uncannily close to middle-class American women's experiences in the suburbs detailed by Friedan.[12]

She's Crazy, Just Crazy

> All he asks of his wife, aside from hours of menial work, is that she not see him as he sees himself. That she not challenge him but admire him, soothe and distract him. In short, make him feel like the kind of guy he'd like to be in the kind of world he thinks exists. (Jones and Brown, 1968, p.12)

In spite of the problems with *The Feminist Mystique*, and the kind of activism it calls for, the book was instrumental in shaping feminist politics of the 1960s. As Horowitz argues: 'As much as any book written in the middle of the twentieth century, *The Feminine Mystique* helped transform the course of America's social and political history [...] By raising the consciousness of legions of women, Friedan assisted in laying the groundwork for their participation in the feminist movement that emerged with increasing force in the late 1960s' (Horowitz, 1998, p.4). *The Feminist Mystique* made Friedan a chief architect and major contributor to the resurgence of the feminist movement in the US. She went on to help found the National Organization for Women in 1966. She founded the National Association for the Repeal of Abortion Laws in 1969 and co-founded the National Women's Political Caucus in 1971 (Fox, 2006). As previously discussed, *The Feminine Mystique* chronicles what Friedan calls 'the problem that has no name' (1963, p.15). She describes this 'problem' as a 'strange stirring, a sense of dissatisfaction, a yearning' felt by middle-class suburban housewives for whom marriage, maternity, and domesticity fail to provide a compelling purpose in life: 'each suburban wife struggled with this alone. As she made the beds, shopped for groceries, matched slip cover material, ate peanut butter sandwiches with her children, chauffeured Cub Scouts and Brownies, lay by her husband at night – she was afraid to ask even of herself the silent question — "Is this all?"' (Friedan, 1963, p.15). Friedan maintains that the silence surrounding this crisis meant that women had no idea if other women shared their anxieties and so they drew conclusions that there must be something individually wrong with them and/or their marriage. According to Friedan, women felt alone, angry, frustrated, completely neurotic, and believed that the only answer was to consult a psychiatrist (Freidan, 1963, p.33). Friedan paints a dramatic picture: in one upper-income suburban development, she interviewed twenty-eight women and discovered that sixteen were receiving psychotherapy, eighteen were taking tranquilisers, several had attempted suicide and some had been hospitalised with mental illness, including psychotic symptoms. She cites a local medical doctor, who (somewhat insensitively) suggests: 'You'd be surprised at the number of these happy suburban wives who simply go berserk one night, and run shrieking through the street without any clothes on' (Friedan, 1963, p.235).

As Joanna and Bobby investigate the strange feminine mystique of Stepford they also begin to doubt their own sanity. They even consider whether there is something in the water – a bio-hazardous chemical spill from a nearby industrial estate. They get a sample tested, but the results conclude that all they have is 'water in their water.' After Bobby becomes victim to the mystique, Joanna is terrified. At that moment, she realises the conspiracy (the problem with no name), but it is impossible to articulate or explain without sounding crazy: 'Her [Bobby's] kitchen is sparkling!' This statement describes horrors known only to Joanna (and the members of the Men's Association). She tries to communicate her fears to Walter who immediately deflects them back onto her. He demands to know when things are going to start sparkling around their home like they suddenly are at Bobby's. He complains that he works eighty hours a week and lives in a great house, but his kids look like they belong on welfare because Joanna dresses them like ragamuffins. He belittles Joanna's burgeoning photography career with the cutting statement, 'if you paid a little more attention to your family and a little less to your god-damn picture taking.' Walter then goes on to demand that she 'see someone – a psychiatrist – because there is something mentally unstable with her' (quoting Walter).

The systematic devaluation of women's grievances through the insistence that they are mentally unbalanced was of concern to many women's rights activists in the 1960s. As Beverly Jones and Judith Brown argue in their influential 1968 manifesto *Towards a Female Liberation Movement*, a typical domestic scenario is for women's complaints to be twisted around by her husband to make her seem senseless: 'She confesses her loneliness, her dependence, her mental agony, and they discuss her problem. *Her problem*, as though it were some genetic defect, some kind of personal shortcoming, some inscrutable psychosis. If she persists she is told that she is crazy, just crazy' (1968, p.12).

The myth that women are inherently prone to mental illness, and the ready diagnosis of disobedient, rebellious, or outspoken women as insane, became common practice in the mid-1800s. It was around this time, following the introduction of the Lunatics Act of 1845 (UK), that there was a shift in approaches to madness. Prior to the Lunatics Act, with the exception of the wealthy and privileged, 'insane' people were sent to public hospitals like Bedlam, or private madhouses where the conditions were appalling and notoriously cruel. Models of confinement focused on punishment and physical restraint. Visitors could pay to see the spectacle of 'howling maniacs,' kept naked in dark reeking cells, strapped down to beds or chairs (Showalter, 1982, p.158). After 1845, the use of force and punishment was officially abolished and replaced by what Michel Foucault describes as the 'domestication of madness' (1965, p.247). Instead of confinement and brutality, behaviour was organised around surveillance and judgement, guilt and self-consciousness. As long as inmates restrained themselves, were agreeable, and did not break the rules (things that all require awareness about one own madness) they would not be subject to constraint. Madness was treated like childishness and inmates were transformed into minors. As Foucault maintains: 'The entire existence of madness, in the world now being prepared for it, was enveloped in what we may call, in anticipation, a "parental complex." The prestige of patriarchy is revived around madness in the bourgeois family' (1965, p.254). This revival of patriarchal power would later be codified by psychoanalysis (Showalter, 1982, p.169).

It was at this time that the number of women in asylums rose significantly. Prior to 1845, men were much more likely to be institutionalised. However, while infirmaries for the criminal insane and 'idiot' schools remained male dominated, women outnumbered men at retreats, large country asylums, and rest-cure homes that were built en mass in the mid-to-late 1800s. By the end of the century, psychiatric physicians began to establish themselves as experts in the 'female illnesses' of hysteria and neurasthenia. In her paper 'Victorian Women and Insanity,' Elaine Showalter explains that women, particularly if they were disobedient, aggressive, or inattentive, were often perceived as displaying signs of an 'unsound mind' and usually felt so guilt ridden about their deviation that they could easily be persuaded to accept psychiatric labels for their emotions and desires: 'Well before Freud and psychoanalysis declared that women were physically deficient and emotionally masochistic beings, Victorian psychiatric theory had evolved to explain mental breakdown in women (or the working class) as evidence of their inferiority' (Showalter, 1982, p.180). Victorian physicians were especially interested in middle-class women who were diagnosed according to a biological model of sex difference and disorders associated with the uterus and reproductive system. Expressions of unhappiness, frustration, low self-esteem, helplessness, anxiety, and fear were connected to the female anatomy, not the realities of women's lives (Showalter, 1982, p.169). Institutionalisation of women by their husbands also became a convenient fashion. Husbands would commonly have their wives committed as a form of domestic abuse and/or so that they could marry someone else. According to Phyllis Chesler, most women in asylums were not insane, though many were talented, stubborn, assertive, or otherwise difficult (2005, p.62).

These histories give context to the myriad of myths and assumptions about women's 'emotional volatility' that have entered cultural lexicon and remain impactful today. In *The Stepford Wives*, Joanna takes on board Walter's accusations that she is mentally unstable and agrees to visit a psychiatrist: the tangible fear and desperation that Joanna experiences when confronted with evidence that something terrible is happening in Stepford is reconfigured, by Walter, as the neurotic ramblings of a

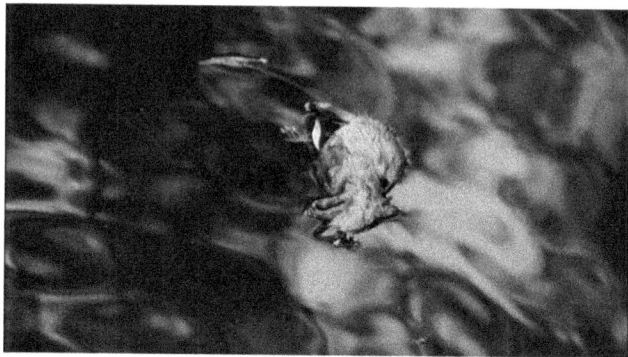

Figure 5: Dead rodent – another forewarning

madwoman – the perfect cover-up. The extended shot of a dead rodent floating in a pond during Joanna's discussion with her therapist is emblematic of how fetid this manipulation of patriarchal power is. It is little wonder that in Freidan's interviews, women readily attributed the problem with no name to insanity: 'The times when I felt that the only answer was to consult a psychiatrist, the times of anger, bitterness and general frustration too numerous to even mention' (Friedan, 1963, p.33).

The subjugation of women and their relegation to the position of mentally unstable 'Other' can be accounted for through the work of philosopher G.W.F Hegel. The notion of the Other finds origin in Hegel's *The Phenomenology of the Spirit* (1807) and his master-slave dialectic, which explores notions of self-identification and self-consciousness. In the master slave relationship, the master only recognises his own selfhood and subjectivity. He objectifies the slave and imposes himself on her/him. Consequently, the slave stops being an autonomous entity. Instead, the slave's self-consciousness is entirely shaped by the master. The slave does not recognise his/her own desires – the only selfhood that exists is that of the master and the master's opinion is all that matters. Hegel's dialectic has been extremely influential to many thinkers, including Simone de Beauvoir, who extrapolates the master/slave power dynamics to sex and the subordination of women by men. de Beauvoir reconceptualises the Hegelian master as the 'subject' and the slave as the 'Other.' Like the master, the subject – men – becomes the naturalised norm by which women are constituted. Therefore, as with the slave, women – the Other – cease to be autonomous entities and are instead framed only in relation to men – the subject

– where they are posited as inferior. These power dynamics operate to maintain patriarchal hegemony. This is also why, according to de Beauvoir, 'woman,' and by extension, any gender, is a historical situation rather than a natural fact – that 'one is not born a woman, rather, one becomes one' (de Beauvoir, 2009, p.38).

Stepford and the Torment of Sisyphus

> Few tasks are more similar to the torment of Sisyphus than those of the housewife; day after day, one must wash dishes, dust furniture, mend clothes that will be dirty, dusty and torn again. The housewife wears herself out running on the spot; she does nothing; she only perpetuates the present. (de Beauvoir, 2009, p.487)
>
> Dale Cobra: 'I like to watch women doing little domestic chores.'
>
> Joanna: 'Well, you came to the right town.'

For second wave feminists, a major weapon in the maintenance of sexual inequality is housework. Friedan states that while she never found a woman who actually fitted the happy housewife image promoted in media and advertising, she did notice that those able to lead lives consistent with the feminine mystique were busy: 'busy shopping, chauffeuring, using their dishwashers and dryers and electric mixers, busy gardening, waxing, polishing, helping with the children's homework, [...] doing thousands of little chores' (Friedan, 1963, p.237). Likewise, fixations with housekeeping are parodied in *The Stepford Wives*. As Joanna quips to Bobby: 'I'm beginning to think there's a nationwide contest I haven't heard about [...]. A million dollars and Paul Newman for the cleanest house by next Christmas. I *mean*, its scrub, scrub, *scrub*; wax, wax, *wax*' (Levin, 1972, p.21). The robot women of Stepford never stop baking, cleaning, and polishing – tasks that apparently need urgent and constant attention, even late into the night, while their husbands are at the Men's Association. When Joanna attempts to revive the once thriving Women's Club (of which Carol was formerly the president) she is met with a wall of resistance. All the wives, aside from Bobby and Charmaine – who are still human at this stage – claim to be too busy, 'what with baking and all that.' When she finally does manage to organise a conscious raising session (after bribing Claude Axhelm), it ends in disaster. Instead of

Figure 6: Dale Cobra watching Joanna do 'little domestic chores'

a lively discussion about sexual discrimination, the conversation resembles a rehearsal for an advertisement for cleaning products. One of the wives – Kit Sunderson (Carole Mallory) – complains that she didn't bake anything the day before because it took her so long to get the upstairs floor to shine. In response, Claude's wife Marie (Toni Reid) launches into a tirade about the time saving properties of 'Easy-On Spray Starch:' 'Well, if time is your enemy, make friends with Easy-On [...] it's so good that if I ever became famous and the Easy-On people asked me to do a commercial, not only would I do it, I'd do it for free – that's how good it is.'

According to Friedan, not only are those living the feminine mystique constantly busy, there was something peculiar about how long it took full time housewives to do domestic chores compared to that of women who perused professions. She claims to have pondered over the question of how one hour of housework could be expanded to fill six hours and came to the conclusion that it was the 'basic paradox of the feminine mystique' (1963, p.238). Housework had become a glorified task. In media, dominant discourse and ideologies promoted housework as glamorous, worthy, and equal to the man's role in society:

> Housework, washing dishes, diaper-changing had to be dressed up by the new mystique to become equal to splitting atoms, penetrating outer space, creating art that illuminates human destiny, pioneering on the frontiers of society. It had to become the very end of life itself to conceal the obvious fact that it is barely the beginning. (Friedan, 1963, p.239)

Freidan attributes the amount of time housewives spend on domestic chores to the theory of 'work expands to fill time available,' conceived by historian C. Northcote Parkinson, based on his experiences with administrative bureaucracy in World War II. According to Freidan, this principle is easily reformulated for the middle-class American housewife to account for why, despite all the laboursaving devices saturating the market in the in the post-war economic boom, technological development had not freed women from the drudgery of cooking, cleaning, and washing (Friedan, 1963, pp.241-2).

For feminist activists, the 'work expands to fill time available' principle also applied to grooming. According to Jones and Brown, because women have been brainwashed by the media to believe their destiny is to find a man and get married, they are also conditioned to think that to get and keep a husband they must spend an inordinate amount of time on how they look: 'the average American woman spends two hours a day in personal grooming, not including shopping or sewing. That is one-twelfth of her whole life and one-eighth of the time she spends awake. If she lives to eighty, a woman will have spent ten whole years of her time awake in this one facet of the complex business of making herself attractive to men' (1968, p.8). They continue, adding: 'it is staggering to think what that figure would be if one were to include the endless hours spent looking through fashion magazines, shopping and window shopping, discussing and worrying about clothes, hair style, diet, and make-up' (1968, p.8).

A central issue for second wave feminist activists was the way that domestic labour, including self-beautification, is used as a weapon to maintain sexual inequality, where the oppression of middle-class women is sustained through myths that the never-ending, time consuming demands of housewifery are somehow of equal importance and urgency to achievements in science, medicine, and high arts. As has been established in this chapter, *The Stepford Wives* presents a powerful critique of these ideologies. The film's interpretation of Friedan's *The Feminine Mystique* and its close engagement with the fundamental points made by Friedan and other feminist activists generates an imposing statement about patriarchal power dynamics and the politics of liberal feminism in the 1960s and 1970s, particularly in relation to myths about happy housewives, marriage, and female agency. However, as this chapter has established, the particular brand of hegemonic feminism Friedan and other white, educated, middle-class women were calling for in the 1960s and 1970s is only relevant to a very narrow demographic. Ignored were the problems of women marginalised by race, class, sexuality, (dis)ability, and other factors. This critique is a more contemporary one, enlightened by the formative works of bell hooks and others. It is not an observation that was made in mainstream media in relation to Friedan's work in 1963 or the film's release in 1975. Further, it does not detract from the value of *The Stepford Wives* as an important historical document in its own right – one that charts a particular moment in gender politics in the US. Instead, it is indicative of vital shifts in thinking that, arguably, would not be taking place if it were not for the formative works of early thinkers like de Beauvoir, and activists such as Friedan.

Chapter 5: *Stepford* Sequels

An important, but overlooked component of the *Stepford* universe is a series of film sequels. During the 1980s and 1990s, three made-for-television follow-ons to *The Stepford Wives* were released: *Revenge of the Stepford Wives*, *The Stepford Children*, and *The Stepford Husbands*. Each of these spin-offs, like the original film, was produced by Edgar J. Scherick Associates. Scherick was also credited as a producer in the 2004 remake of the film. *Revenge of the Stepford Wives* originally screened on NBC on 12 October as part of 'The Big Event' – a prime-time weekly movie premier occasion courtesy of the 'NBC theatre.' *The Stepford Children* was also released on NBC (broadcasting on 15 March 1987). *The Stepford Husbands* was made for CBS (airing 14 May 1996). It is easy to overlook the significance of these films. The plot lines are rather rudimentary and they follow much more clichéd horror trajectories, but on closer analysis they, like the original *Stepford Wives*, offer some interesting insight into particular social, cultural, and political dynamics taking place at the time of their production, especially in relation to gender politics. Thus, as a collective they from an integral part of the *Stepford* universe. This chapter will unpack the critical themes underpinning each of these films. It will explore the way they engage with dominant discourses and ideologies circulating in mainstream media and popular culture during the 1980s and 1990s. As part of this analysis, the chapter will also explore parallels between the *Stepford* universe and 1950s alien invasion films, which have a shared ancestry in the articulation of anxieties about shifting gender relations, disruptions to hegemonic masculinity, and suburbanisation.

Happy Pills and Payback

Revenge of the Stepford Wives opens by informing the audience that the setting is 'Stepford – 10 years later,' implying a direct continuation of Forbes' film. It then shows a couple attempting to flee the town because 'the wife is not adjusting,' only to have their car forced off a cliff by the local sheriff. This establishes an ominous pretext for the rest of the production: Stepford is a place where no one leaves. The central protagonist is a reporter called Kaye Foster (Sharon Gless) who comes to Stepford to investigate why the town has such low rates of reported crime, divorce, and real-estate turnover. She immediately attracts a lot of negative attention, particularly from head of the Men's Association: Dale 'Diz' Corbett (Arthur Hill) – this film's equivalent of Dale Cobra. Kaye is subject to police surveillance and one of the wives tries to murder her, twice. She quickly becomes friends with a dynamic, undomesticated 'Bobby counterpart' called Megan Brady (Julie Kavner), who is new to Stepford and living in the same motel as Kaye with her husband Andy (Don Johnson) – a probationary police officer. Kaye and Megan are stark contrasts to the other women of Stepford, who are all robotically one-dimensional, anachronistic, and obsessed with housework, just as they are in the original movie. They are also costumed in the same style of long, flowing, pastel coloured gowns and broad brimmed floppy hats – a clear homage to Forbes' film.

However, there are a number of significant differences between this production and the original, the most pronounced being that the wives are not murdered and replaced by robots. Instead, they are brainwashed and chemically automated with heavy 'thyroid' prescription drugs that they must take four times a day. To remind them a loud communal siren sounds, adding to the prison-like quality of the town. The ongoing maintenance involved in the zombification of the wives implies that it is reversible. Indeed, after Megan is chemically lobotomised following a 'medical assessment' for insurance purposes, Kay is able to isolate her and eventually undo the effects of the drugs and mental programming. Reading the film from a feminist perspective, the concept of reversibility suggests hope – that women may well have been indoctrinated into wanting nothing more than 'a husband, split level house, three children, a dog, a cat, and a station wagon' (Jones and Brown, 1968, p.8), but they are not doomed to the feminine mystique as the original *Stepford Wives* suggests. Further, as the inclusion of the word 'revenge' in the title insinuates, the wives of Stepford get retribution for the way they have been treated. Kaye sabotages the siren system, interfering with the wives' medication schedule. This somehow alters their constitutional state, transforming them into angry avengers. They storm the Men's Association and throw Dale Corbett out of a second-story window. In the closing scene the wives surround Corbett as he lies on the ground. The camera adopts his visual perspective as the women kick and stomp their master oppressor to death – symbolically stamping out the misogyny and conservatism that has sanctioned their abuse, rape and objectification for so long: a radical feminist reaction in keeping with calls to action declared in manifestos like *Towards a Female Liberation Movement*:

> Men have accelerated their rate of history-making beyond humane proportions. With their slaves secure at home, they have the time to play abstractly and inhumanely with their technology and to make history more rapidly than they can effectively comprehend or control [...]. The goal of the new left is to dismantle outworn institutions and replace them with better arrangements [...]. Women mobilized where they stand against the nearest oppressor, will make their most effective contribution to this process. (Jones and Brown, 1968, pp.24-5)

The mid-to-late 1970s (just prior to the broadcast of *Revenge*) was also a time when mainstream media started to sensationalise the overuse of prescription medication by middle-class housewives, creating a state of 'Valium panic.' Articles appearing in magazines like Vogue began warning of the habit-forming properties of drugs like Diazepam, dramatically declaring them to be more addictive and harder to withdraw from than heroine and morphine.[13] This US Food and Drug Administration (FDA) announcement cautions of 'junkies' hiding in plain sight in the suburbs:

> The smartly dressed woman driving a sleek, late model car could be the envy of her neighbours. She has a loving husband, bright children, a beautiful home in the suburbs, and apparently no cares in the world. Except one. This woman is a junkie. She's not the kind of junkie one thinks of in terms of long-haired 'hippies,' counter-culture street people, pushers, and illicit drugs. She's dependent on legal drugs, the kind prescribed for her by a physician. ('Tranquilizers: Use, Abuse, and Dependency,' *FDA Consumer*, October 1978, 21 – cited in Herzberg, 2010, p.122)

The use of psychotropic drugs instead of animatronic technology to turn women into 'robots' in *Revenge* is telling of the socio-cultural dynamics involving prescription medications at the time. According to David Herzberg in his book *Happy Pills in America* (2010), epidemiological studies and drug utilisation surveys conducted in the 1960s and 1970s consistently revealed that women were using tranquilisers at twice the rate of men, and in large quantities (Valium alone was being dispensed at a rate of 90 million bottles per annum by the 1970s). Consequently, tranquilisers and antidepressants came to be viewed as 'women's drugs.' However, in popular media, before cautions like the above cited FDA message emerged, this was not seen as a problem. Quite the contrary, psychotropics were viewed as a *solution* to women's 'inherently neurotic tendencies,' enabling them to resume their 'traditional' housewifery roles and revive their feminine qualities of submissiveness, nurturance, and familial devotion (Herzberg, 2010, p.73). Drug advertising promoted the notion that America's middle-class housewives, with their white-collar husbands, were riddled with anxiety and neurosis. They promised that pills could return women to happiness in homemaker settings and restore their supposedly natural ability to serve others, particularly their family. In essence, tranquilisers could help women achieve the patriarchal ideal of the feminine mystique.

Advertisement for psychotropics did not just sell drugs to women, they promoted housewifery as a normative role. For example, in an advert originally appearing in the *Journal of the American Medical Association* (*JAMA*, July 16 1960) for a popular tranquilizer called Meprospan, a white, middle-class housewife is shown consulting a physician, where she explains that she feels tense and nervous. She is prescribed two Meprospan capsules per day. The first enables her to stay calm, 'even under the pressure of busy, crowded supermarket shopping' and to remain 'alert, relaxed, and attentive' at parent teacher meetings. The second capsule helps her sleep peacefully at night, 'undisturbed by nervousness or tension' (Herzberg, 2010, p.77). Another advert from *JAMA* (April 13 1970) for the antidepressant Vivactil promises to 'first get the patient moving' – accompanied by an image of a woman lugging an overflowing laundry basket down the basement stairs – 'then gets her mood improving.' This second statement shows a close-up shot of a woman smiling salaciously into the camera using direct address (Herzberg, 2010, p.78). Other drug promotions go further, explicitly identifying dissatisfaction with housewifery itself as an illness. For instance, a 1970s advert for the antidepressant Sinequan medicalises marital unhappiness by listing it along with a number of physical symptoms as part of the patient's underlying mental disorder. The advert shows a woman standing forlornly next to a washing line full of clothes with her head stooped and her hands clasped together in front of her. The caption reads: 'A lot of little things are wrong.

Headaches, diarrhoea, this rash on my arm. And sometimes I think I don't like being married.' This statement blatantly suggests that unhappiness in being a housewife is an individual problem that can be solved if women 'readjust' their situation, possibly with the use of pills (Herzberg, 2010, pp.81-2). Further, it is demonstrative of the kind of rhetoric that Friedan critiques in *The Feminine Mystique*. As established in Chapter 4, Friedan also identified middle-class housewives as riddled with anxiety and neurosis – 'the problem that has no name' (1963, p.15). However, Friedan diverges from drug companies and gender traditionalists through her argument that women's sufferings were not medical phenomena to be relieved by psychotropic drugs, but a 'political problem to be cured through social change' (Herzberg, 2010, p.79). For Friedan, pills were a convenient device for the social and medical forces that kept housewives in their place: 'Her anxiety can be soothed by therapy, or tranquilized by pills, or evaded temporarily by busywork. But her unease, her desperation, is nonetheless a warning that her human existence is in danger, even though she has found fulfilment, according to the tenets of the feminine mystique, as a wife and mother' (Friedan, 1963, p.314).

Stepford Husbands and Backlash

Revenge of the Stepford Wives offers a poignant critique of dominant discourses promoting 'mother's little helper'[14] as a solution to housewife dissatisfaction and the problem that has no name. Interestingly, *The Stepford Husbands* also exchanges sci-fi solutions found in the original film for pharmacologically grounded ones, in this case to chemically automate the wayward husbands of Stepford, who are all invariably diagnosed with 'male dissociative disorder.' *The Stepford Husbands* gender flips *The Stepford Wives*, reinventing Stepford as a town controlled by a powerful female scientist who operates a clinic specialising in the treatment of 'problematic' husbands. Instead of Men's Association meetings there are 'ladies only power breakfasts' where women's career pursuits are actively endorsed and celebrated. The film centres on a New York couple Jodie and Mick Davidson (played by Donna Mills and Michael Ontkean). Jodie is a high-profile career woman and Mick is a struggling screenwriter. The move to Stepford (for a new start) is initiated by Jodie who has a friend that lives there. Mick reluctantly agrees, but as the narrative progresses he becomes increasingly dissatisfied with the transition and starts to act up, just like an unruly teenager – bouncing his basketball around the house while Jodie is trying to work, drinking excessively, throwing temper tantrums, and smashing things.

Jodie's friend Lisa (Caitlin Clarke) suggests she consult Dr Frances Borzage (Sarah Douglas), the founder of the Stepford Clinic for Problem Men. Lisa's husband Gordon (Jeffrey Pillars) was recently admitted to Dr. Borzage's treatment centre, remerging as a seemingly idyllic husband and father. Dr Borzage explains to Jodie:

> The last 25 years have been a period of revolutionary change for men and women. Women have careers, they have money, they have power. We want men who are going to protect us. This can be very confusing for them. Many men find themselves struggling to fit into a world that they really don't understand. Feeling isolated they are torn between positions of power and powerlessness and [sigh] sometimes they lash out – the anger – male dissociative disorder.

Dr Borzage questions how women are able to have it all when they have difficult husbands like this to look after too. Her solution is to transform men into 'perfect' partners who can serve women instead of hinder them. This sounds appealing to Jodie, so she has Mick committed to the clinic where he is strapped to a gurney and intravenously pumped full of drugs. On his release he is given a potent concoction of stimulants, steroids, hormones, serotonin reuptake inhibitors (SSRIs), and tranquilisers that he must take with meals and before bed. He is certainly calmer and better behaved, but sex with him is dull and robotic. There are other problems with the therapy too. Jodie discovers that the family who lived in her house before her were massacred by the husband after he underwent treatment at Dr Borzage's centre. Similarly, Gordon displays indicators of latent fury towards his own children, hinting that he is close to having a murderous outburst as well. The drug concoction may stupefy the men, but it merely masks their patriarchal rage, and in fact, might even make it worse. Dr Borzage is presented as a cold, sinister, and power hungry. The Stepford women's need to 'have it all' – career, independence, a family – is depicted as selfish and ultimately deadly since the chemically lobotomized men they create lash back. Hence, in stark contrast to the original film, *The Stepford*

Husbands effectively problematizes and undermines the goals of feminism, actively engaging with postfeminist discourses and ideologies that first became prominent in mainstream media in the early 1990s.

While the term postfeminism is complex and loaded with contradictions, most academic thinkers concede that central to the underlying agenda of postfeminism is the desire to restabilise gender power structures that have been disrupted by the political, economic, and legislative gains of earlier feminist movements (see Projansky, 2001; McRobbie, 2009; Tasker & Negra, 2009, for instance). Crucially, postfeminism is distinct in that unlike feminism, it does not function as a way of giving voice to the collective concerns of women. Nor does it seek to challenge male hegemony. Instead, postfeminism is a patriarchally grounded, media inspired concept that promotes the individualistic, consumer driven rhetoric of neoliberalism, while shying away from, or superficially engaging with, political discourse (Lindop, 2015, p.11). According to Susan Faludi, who is well known for her book *Backlash: The Undeclared War against Women* (1991), the term postfeminism is inspired by the concept that the feminist project was, by the 1980s, dead (Faludi, 1991, p.101). This assertion is based on the premise that feminist activism of the 1960s and 1970s was no longer needed since women had achieved sexual equality and independence. However, not only did the media espouse the belief that feminism was now unnecessary, there was also a more insidious idea, promoted by mainstream discourses, that feminism was actually destructive to the lives of women. Faludi describes this process as a 'backlash against feminism' (1991, p.103). As Faludi argues, rhetoric began circulating in media that feminism had been a 'great experiment' that had not only failed, but caused a crisis. Although bearing little relation to the actual lives of women, the desire to 'have-it-all' was blamed for making them selfish, miserable, and unhealthy (Faludi, 1991, pp.2-9; Negra, 2007, p.2; Projansky, 2001, p.116).

Though Faludi's backlash thesis is influential, it has since been critiqued for its lack of complexity in that it fails to address the diverse relationship between feminism, femininity, and popular culture. As prominent theorist Angela McRobbie argues, rather than feminism simply being rejected, what more accurately occurs in popular culture is that elements of feminism are simultaneously taken into account and repudiated in a process that McRobbie describes as 'double entanglement': 'postfeminism positively draws on and evokes feminism [...] to suggest that equality has been achieved, in order to install a whole new repertoire of meaning which emphasises that it is no longer needed, that it is a spent force' (McRobbie, 2009, p.12). Hence, according to Anthea Taylor (2012, p.13), what is indicative of postfeminism is a tension created by the endorsement, even celebration of feminism, and its simultaneous disavowal: contradictions that are, as Taylor suggests, 'constitutive of postfeminism itself' (2012, p.13). These dynamics are transparently played out in *The Stepford Husbands*, which places a premium on women's right to career and independence, but at the same time renders it toxic. Hence, by 1996, the town of Stepford has become ground zero for feminism's great failed experiment.

Much of the popularity of themes involving successful career women turned sinister psychopath can be attributed to the success of *Fatal Attraction* (Adrian Lyne, 1987) – a film that paved the way for this kind of representation. Maniacal career woman Alex Forrest (played by Glenn Close, who also stars as Stepford's mad scientist and Dr Borzage equivalent in Frank Oz's 2004 take on *The Stepford Wives*) is not only a psychotic stalker who becomes unhinged after the married man she is having an affair with rejects her, she is also a desperate woman whose career aspirations have, as Faludi puts it, 'precluded her marital success and left her envying the connubial pleasures found in the domestic sphere' (1991, p.3). Alex launches a systematic attack on her lover's good, stay-at-home wife and mother: a fight that Alex loses, paying for it with her life.[15] Crucially, where feminist films like the original *Stepford Wives* was actively critiquing dominant discourses concerning the idealisation and promotion of housewifery as a source of domestic bliss, by the 1990s the feminine mystique was again held up in media as an ideal version of femininity and happiness.

Stepford Children, Patriarchal Rage, and Alien Invasion

The Stepford Husbands does not only articulate a failure of feminism through engagement with popular postfeminist ideologies, it also expresses it via depictions of patriarchal impotence and rage; a theme indicative of broader trends in the horror genre that began to emerge in the late-1970s and 1980s and a form of backlash in its own right. As Vivian Sobchack identifies, this era saw moves to single out fathers as the primary negative force in the middle-class family: 'It is in the late 1970s that the genre begins to overtly interrogate paternity and its relation to patriarchal power' (1986, p.13). In the 1960s, husbands like Guy Woodhouse in *Rosemary's Baby* were willing to relinquish paternity in a pact with the devil for success and fame. However, by the late-1970s, fathers were not just weak and materialistic, they were furious. As Sobchack suggests: 'we can see in *Rosemary's Baby* the radical beginning of patriarchal failure: of paternity refused, denied, abandoned, hated; of patriarchy simultaneously terrified and terrorising in the fact of its increasing impotence; of patriarchy maddened by a paradoxical desire for its own annihilation' (1986, p.14).

Prominent examples include possessed, axe wielding George Lutz (James Brolin) in *Amityville Horror* (Stuart Rosenberg, 1979). *Amityville* is not just about a haunted middle-class home; it also involves an obsessed middle-class father and husband who, weak under economic pressure from his corrupt and demanding dream home, turns on his family (Sobchack, 1986, pp.13-14). Kubrick's 1980 cinematic adaption of Stephen King's *The Shining* (1980) is another illustration. Here patriarchal rage is explicit and ironically realised in the leering, abusive hatred of Jack Torrance (Jack Nicholson), a struggling writer like Mike Davidson, who projects his fury onto his loved ones. Similarly, in *The Stepfather* (1987), Jerry Blake (Terry O'Quinn) is a deranged psychopath who makes a career of marrying into readymade, fatherless families, only to later slaughter them as soon as they fail to live up to his idealistic expectations.

Patriarchal rage is also seething in *The Stepford Children*. This sequel deploys the fundamental premise of the original narrative involving a move away from the transgressive metropolitan lifestyle of Manhattan, to a quieter, more 'family friendly' existence in Stepford, Connecticut: a transition initiated by the father of a traditional nuclear family, in this case the Hardings – Laura (Barbara Eden), who is a lawyer preparing for her bar exam, Steven (Don Murray) and their adolescent children Mary (Tammy Lauren) and David (Randall Batinkoff). The film makes clear from the outset that the men of Stepford are not only replacing their wives with robots, but now that their children have grown into obnoxious teenagers (in keeping with the twelve-year gap between Forbes' film and this 1987 sequel), they are abducting them and substituting them for androids too. It is also made evident that Steven has lived in Stepford before, with his first wife Karen, who died mysteriously (Laura later digs up her grave to reveal it occupied by a robot). Like the original film, the Hardings are not the only new family in Stepford. The Gregsons are also recent arrivals. Sandy Gregson (Sharon Spelmon) is an energetic, motorbike riding dynamo, Lois Gregson (Debbie Barker), the daughter, is a sexually confident teenager, and Frank Gregson (Ken Swofford), the husband/father, is an aggressive domestic despot. The narrative plays out a high-tension 'who's next' scenario with Sharon and Lois the first to be exchanged for hyper-conservative, ultra-conformist facsimiles. The storyline becomes a little messy following Mary's replacement after an 'evening out' with her father. The next morning her appearance and behaviour are radically different. Gone is her soft-core punk aesthetic. Instead, she presents as an ideal of Victorian sensibilities. Laura is immediately suspicious and confronts Mary, who attacks her with a large carving knife. In an ensuing struggle, Mary is thrown to the floor where she short circuits. Laura then makes her way to the Men's Association where she finds the real Mary restrained, but still alive in a greenhouse type laboratory. Surrounding her are a number of gelatinous humanoid creatures attached to tubes. These quasi-embryotic beings are strikingly similar to the developing human doppelgangers in Don Siegel's 1956 classic horror *Invasion of the Body Snatchers*. Interestingly, Forbes' The *Stepford Wives* was compared to alien invasion narratives on its release. One review appearing in *The Independent Film Journal* describes it as 'a cross between *Invasion of the Body Snatchers* and a women's liberation fairy tale' (19 Feb 1975 pp. 75-6).

Invasion of the Body Snatchers is part of the post-World War II alien invasion film cycle, along with other classic sci-fi horrors like *The Day the Earth Stood Still, Invaders from Mars, It Came from Outer Space*, and *I Married a Monster from Outer Space* (Gene Fowler, 1958) to name just a few. *Invasion of the Body Snatchers* is set in a small town called Santa Mira, California where the film's protagonist, Dr Miles Bennell (Kevin McCarthy), realises that aliens are taking over the people around him. These extraterrestrials kill their hosts after producing clones of them in what look like giant pea pods. The clones are noticeable because of their flattened affect – 'they have no need for love, desire, ambition, faith.' In essence, they are robotic. The aliens waste no time in taking over the entire town, seizing control of the police force and other government officials. They then begin to ship their pods to other towns, presumably with the intention of taking over the country and eventually the world.

Invasion of the Body Snatchers has been interpreted as a cautionary tale about the creeping totalitarianism of the McCarthy era; a commentary on the suburban conformity of the Eisenhower years; and a protest against the effects of mass industrialisation (Hendershot, 1998, pp.30-33; Vizzini 'Cold War' p.30). It can equally be read as an expression of Cold War paranoia with the aliens bearing a striking resemblance to common American stereotypes of communists as lacking individualism and possessing a hive mind (Vizzini pp.29-30). Similarly, *Invaders from Mars* and *I Married a Monster from Outer Space* can be seen as a vindication of anti-communist hysteria. In *Invaders from Mars*, a boy called David Maclean (Jimmy Hunt) witnesses a spaceship crash near his home. On David's insistence, his father George (Leif Erickson) goes to investigate the crash. When he returns sometime later he is cold, cruel, and robotic – opposite to the warm, loving man that he was before. Soon the entire town including David's mother, friends, the police and the army are all converted to drone-like Martian agents. In *I Married a Monster*, the aliens invade small town America, but in this case, they only target men. Their plan is to replace all human males and inseminate Earth women with alien hybrids who will mindlessly obey their extraterrestrial masters. This speaks back to socio-cultural tensions concerning post-war immigration. In awareness of the horrors of the Nazi death camps, the US increased its migration quotas following WWII, leading to a large influx of refugees from Europe. But as Edwin Harwood (1986) explains in his survey of US immigration policies, prevailing public opinion remained staunchly restrictionist – a nationalistic concept of community traceable back to the Civil War. The emergence of America as a major industrial power in the late 1800s fuelled this attitude, giving rise to aggressive ideologies of national dominance that remained well into the 1950s. With these dynamics in mind *I Married a Monster* can be viewed as a paranoid warning about immigrant assimilation and especially marrying foreign men.

I Married a Monster can equally be seen as allegory for 1950s fears that male veterans returning from the war might be suffering from unknown mental instabilities after being brutalised in battle – that they may come home as 'strangers' and 'aliens' within their families (see Cathy Hawkins, 2004, p.37). In the film, the protagonist's husband-to-be goes out with friends on the eve of their wedding, but returns with a different personality. He is cold, distant and ignores the protagonist Marge (Gloria Talbott). He shows no desire to spend time with her, even on their honeymoon, and disappears from the house on a nightly basis. This is a very similar theme to the one at the centre of *Invaders from Mars*, where David's father returns a changed person. As well as relating to fears about immigration and post-World War II traumatic stress, *Invaders from Mars* and *I Married a Monster* also articulate tensions about living in suburbia and the idea that lurking just behind the idyllic façade of domestic bliss are disturbing familial secrets.

Yet another reading of alien invasion films is that they are metaphor for 'white fright.' This again relates to anxieties about suburbia. Eric Avila describes white fright as the processes by which American cities of the post-war period saw increasing racial segregation and socioeconomic fragmentation (2005, p.88). Communists were not the only subversives of post-war America – synonymous with new suburban enclaves of the 1950s was the preservation of whiteness: 'Through post-war collusion of federal policy, local land development strategies, and the popular desire to live in racially exclusive and homogenous neighbourhoods, "chocolate" cities and "vanilla" suburbs became the spatial and racial paradigm of American life' (Avila, 2005, p.88). The 1950s Hollywood alien invasion zeitgeist paralleled post-war white exoduses to the suburbs. It is easy to see the allegorical alignment to white preoccupations with racial Otherness.

While *The Stepford Wives* and its sequels involve themes of replacement, alteration, and zombification, those that have been substituted are not the threat like they are in alien invasion films. Instead, the threat comes from inside the home, from the people who are closest and most trusted. Foremost, this speaks back to anxieties about the disintegration of traditional gender order. Especially resonant in the sequels are patriarchal anxieties that manifest as a backlash against feminism; both in the form of patriarchal rage and postfeminist logic that undermines many of the gains of feminism. Hence, like the original *Stepford Wives*, the sequels are revealed to be a product of the socio-cultural climate of their creation. By the 1980s, significant shifts in gender politics were beginning to take place – particularly the mobilisation of neoliberalism as a political ideology, and with it, the emergence of postfeminist discourses in media and popular culture. These shifting agendas manifest in the narrative focus of the *Stepford* follow-ons, especially *The Stepford Husbands*, which was made at a time when postfeminism had gained particularly strong traction. Consequently, this examination of the *Stepford* sequels provides important context for the analysis of the *Stepford* remake, which is the focus of the next chapter.

Chapter 6: *The Stepford* Remake – from Sci-Fi Thriller to Farce?

I fucked up. [..] I played it safe. For the first time I didn't follow my instincts. And what happened was, I had too much money, and I was too responsible and concerned for Paramount. I was too concerned for the producers. And I didn't follow my instinct, which I hold as sacred usually. I love being subversive and dangerous, and I wasn't. I was safe, and as a result my decisions were all over the place, and it was my fault totally. (Frank Oz in an interview with *Ain't It Cool* [Merrick, 2007] on why his version of *The Stepford Wives* was not well received)

The Stepford sequels (discussed in Chapter 5) rework Forbes' production in various ways, but one common thread is a shift away from sci-fi, towards a greater emphasis on more straightforward themes of suspense and horror. Alternatively, Oz's re-imagining of *The Stepford Wives* picks up the original's sci-fi focus, gothic sensibilities, and dark, satirical humour, but lampoons it. The result is a romantic-comedy, come kitschy, camp exercise in hyperbolic excess. As critic Lisa Nuss asserts, the 2004 remake 'has changed from thriller to farce, making for plenty of audience laughs, but also sacrificing the heart of the original movie' (Nuss, 2004). Nuss goes on to point out that the film dredges up many of the insults flung at ambitious women who choose to follow their career dreams and challenges the myth that deep down, women are happiest while taking care of the home. Alissa Quart (2004) describes *Stepford Wives* remake as a 'droll but toothless comedy' and a 'patched together amusement.' Indeed, the majority of reviews, both academic and journalistic, comment that the parody employed in the film not only sacrifices the heart of the original movie, but renders it virtually unintelligible (Johnston and Sears, 2011; Griffin, 2004; Leonard, 2007).

Unlike the original, which was wholly invested in political feminist commentary, offering a scathing critique of patriarchal hegemony and the marginalisation of women, version two is imbued with postfeminist discourses and ideologies. In the same vein as *The Stepford Husbands*, *The Stepford Wives* remake vilifies ambitious women who aspire to both a successful career and family life, implying that the desire to 'have it all' is the sole reason for familial disintegration, making *women* the problem. The film holds up the feminine mystique (as described by Friedan) as an ideal. But at the same time – as is indicative of postfeminism – it offers conflicting messages about gender power relations and the position of women in society. Like A. O. Scott points out in a review for *The New York Times* (2004), the film shirks social criticism, pulling back into homily and reassurance, soothing anxieties rather than provoking them, making it the opposite of satire and the inverse of the original *Stepford Wives*. Similarly, Natasha Forrest, writing for *the F word* comments: 'For a film that claims to be criticising or at least mocking backlash, it certainly does a good job of playing up to society's worst fears of feminism […] satire just becomes meaningless in the context of a film which seems unwilling, afraid or simply too confused to commit to any particular ideology or viewpoint' (2004).

The Stepford Wives version two opens with montage of original 1950s vintage advertising and film footage showing women celebrating domesticity and exulting state of the art household appliances – ovens, washing machines, fridges, vacuum cleaners, toasters, rotisseries, and more. These images suggest nostalgia for a time when women aspired to the mystique of femininity.[16] Cut to a large promotional event where Joanna (Nicole Kidman) – president of a TV network EBS – enthusiastically vaunts two new gameshows. The first, *Balance of Power*, pits heterosexual couples against each other in a 'battle of the sexes' scenario reminiscent of popular media showdowns of the 1960s and 1970s. However, instead of a tennis match, the competition rests on who is fastest to hit the buzzer in response to questions like 'who makes more money?', 'who enters ironman triathlons every year and wins?' and 'who secretly wishes they were married to a hot, sexy, lesbian?' (the latter question being the only one the man bothers to responds to). The second gameshow, *I Can Do Better*, sends a married couple (separately) to a tropical island full of 'professional prostitutes.' Husband Hank (Mike White) admits that he loves his wife Barbara (Carrie Preston) and remained faithful to her the entire time. On the other hand Barbara, who spent the weekend having sex with multiple people, comes to the conclusion that she can do better than Hank.

Suddenly, Hank appears in person at the promotional event. Raging over his wife's rejection of him, he proposes a new gameshow of his own called *Let's Kill All the Women*, before firing a gun multiple times at Joanna. It is later revealed that Hank

The Stepford Wives

also shot his ex-wife and five of her lovers. On the back of this, the EBS executives decide to fire Joanna. Traumatised, she barely makes it to the elevator before having a complete nervous breakdown. The following scene shows her husband Walter (Mathew Broderick) visiting dishevelled Joanna in hospital where he informs her that he has quit his job at EBS (after all, he is only a vice president). Questioning the kind of woman she has become, Joanna asks if they can start over. Hence, the family relocates to Stepford. In this rendition, the Eberharts are driving a Mercedes rather than a station wagon and Stepford is an exclusive gated community filled with lush, opulent mansions shot in soft focus. The colour palette of Stepford is rich and warm, offering a stark contrast to Manhattan, with its cool blue/grey hues and abundance of glass and concrete. This creates an impression of Stepford as a fantasy location akin to a theme park.

The overarching narrative structure is loosely similar to the original text, though, as Oz asserts in the DVD extras, the supermarket scene is the only actual homage to Forbes' work. The husbands are incredibly wealthy Silicon Valley types who spend all their time hanging out at the Men's Association. They drive an assortment of vintage muscle cars, luxury sports cars, Harley Davidson motorbikes, and essentially behave like juvenile frat boys. According to Oz, 'the men really are idiots, they're twits. They're frightened to death of strong women.' Hence, the desire to turn their wives into remote-controlled sex robots. While the head of the Men's Association is a creepy former Microsoft guru called Mike Wellington (Christopher Walken), it is his wife Claire (Glenn Close) who seems to control the entire town. She manages everything from the real-estate, to barn dances, to 'Clairebotics' fitness classes held at the Stepford Day Spa, where the women, costumed in 1950s style dresses, pretend to be washing machines.

Towards the end of the film, it is divulged that it is actually Claire who is the puppet master of Stepford. After Joanna knocks Mike's head off, revealing him to be a robot, Claire confesses that she used to be the world's foremost brain surgeon and genetic engineer: 'I had top secret contracts with The Pentagon, Apple, and Mattel. I was driven, exhausted, until I came home to find Mike with Patricia, my brilliant, blonde, twenty-one-year-old Research Assistant – it was all so ugly.' So Claire murdered them both and built a copy of Mike – the perfect man. She envisaged Stepford as an ideal

Figure 7: Mad scientist Claire (Glenn Close)

place where 'men are men and women are cherished and loved: a world of romance and beauty, of tuxedos and chiffon.'

Postfeminist Popular Culture and Oz's *Stepford*

This romanticism of suburban towns – and of traditionalism – is indicative of postfeminist discourses at the beginning of the twenty-first century. As Diane Negra argues, postfeminist popular culture in the late 1990s and early 2000s was especially obsessed with women retreating from urban environments and high powered careers to find happiness and fulfilment in traditionalist roles and 'hometown' settings:

> It has become common practice for the female protagonist of the contemporary romantic comedy to abjure an urban environment, "downshifting" her career or ambitions in order to re-prioritize family commitments and roles [...]. Early 2000s films frequently conjoin self-discovery with the rejection of the city. Recent chick flicks routinely depict urban professional women whose crisis of identity are linked to a dawning realization that they cannot truly be at home in the urban milieu. (Negra, 2009, pp.18-19)

These themes are central to *The Stepford Wives* remake. Joanna's career is apparently placing an insurmountable strain on her marriage. An exasperated Walter asserts that Joanna's dominating attitude makes people want to kill her – the subtext being that it is her fault she was shot at and sacked from her job, deflecting culpability away from Hank who is, after all, just a man pushed to breaking point by female emancipation. Walter goes on to complain that Joanna is so busy running the television network they have not had sex in a year and her children do not even know her. He comments on her choice to wear black all the time: 'only high-powered, neurotic, castrating Manhattan career bitches wear black. Is that what you want to be?' to which Joanna responds: 'Ever since I was a little girl.' Crucially, Joanna also concedes that her drive to be 'the smartest of the smart' is a problem; that she too is miserable; and importantly, that she loves Walter and does not want him to leave her (as he threatens to do). Hence, she promises to embrace the 'hometown' lifestyle and be the family focused, cup-cake baking, pastel wearing, wife and mother Walter wants. As Negra suggests, 'the popular cultural landscape has seldom been as dominated as it is today by fantasies and fears about women's "life choices"' (2009, p.2). The postfeminist subject is represented repeatedly as having lost herself but then (re)achieving stability through romance (Negra, 2009, p.5).[17] Negra draws on rom-coms such as *Sweet Home Alabama* (Andy Tennant, 2002), *Serendipity* (Peter Chelsom, 2001), and *Kate & Leopold* (James Mangold, 2001) as examples. *The Stepford Wives* also plugs into classic rom-com tropes that offer love and romance as the sole source of certainty and redemption.

As established in Chapter 5, postfeminism is considered a response to feminist activism. It both endorses and problematises feminism depending on the neoliberal political agenda it is serving. According to Negra, postfeminist discourses are prone to caricaturing, distorting, and wilfully misunderstanding the political and social goals of feminism. Often this involves trading on the notion of feminism as 'rigid, serious, anti-sex and romance, difficult and extremist. In contrast, postfeminism offers the pleasure and comfort of (re) claiming identity uncomplicated by gender politics, postmodernism, or institutional critique' (Negra, 2009, p.2). Oz's version of *The Stepford Wives* caricaturises Joanna as an extreme product of feminism: an over-ambitious, obsessed, 'career bitch' who dominates all situations, demands perfection, and prioritises her profession over everything, including sex. This severe version of womanhood is rigorously problematised and rendered intolerable throughout the film.

Like *Revenge of the Stepford Wives*, the women are not actually murdered and replaced. Rather they are re-programmed *vis-à-vis* Mike's 'Female Improvement System.' This is introduced to Walter and Joanna using a retro-inspired promotional video showing a gloomy, unkempt, primitive looking woman with sagging breasts who is picked up by her husband and loaded into a pink, dome-shaped machine. Here Nano chips, sugar, and spice are implanted into her brain and she comes out looking like a *Playboy* Bunny. Also like *Revenge*, this transformation process is reversible. Walter ultimately decides that he does not want a wife who presents as a Barbie doll and behaves like a slave. During a ballroom extravaganza, where Joanna pretends to have been Nano-chipped, Walter sneaks into the Men's Association science laboratory and activates the 'Nano-reversal process,' transforming all the wives and token gay character Roger Bannister (Roger Bart) back to their original selves. Hence, as much as the film ridicules high-powered career women, it also mocks Claire Wellington's nostalgic fantasies about a world uncomplicated by feminism – something some women apparently want as much as men. This is compounded by Claire's pathetic demise after she is electrocuted while kissing Mike's severed head. As is indicative of postfeminism, the film scorns both the traditional homemaker and the career focused wife/mother. However, these contradictions also seem to be resolved. In a final scene, Joanna, along with Bobby (Bette Midler) and Roger, are being interviewed by talk show host Larry King about their recent successes. Joanna has just produced a multi-Emmy Award winning documentary called *Stepford: The Secret of the Suburbs*. King notes that Walter, who is standing just off set with the couple's children in tow, really came through for Joanna. He asks if everything is perfect between them. Joanna responds by clarifying that they are not perfect, because perfect doesn't work. Instead, they are doing just great. Joanna's appearance has also softened. Her hair is now blonde not dark brown, and she is wearing aubergine not black. This suggests that Joanna has satisfied her high-achiever needs, but has also learned to be a 'good wife,' while not succumbing wholly to the feminine mystique. As Imelda Whelehan suggests in reference to the film: 'It is as if postfeminism's schizophrenic logic at once situates men at the heart to the "problem" in women's lives, but cannot condemn them or represent them changing, for fear of offering an authentic (and therefore dangerous) feminist critique' (2010, p.170).

Postfeminism and Techno-Anxiety in *Stepford II*

As much as Oz's remake is grounded in postfeminist ideology, it is also preoccupied with imaginings about techno-science. As has been established in previous chapters, scientific mastery and the conflation of women with technology has to do with gender power relations and the maintenance of patriarchal domination. The men of Stepford are obsessed with gadgets and electronic innovation that extend beyond governing their wives bodies and actions with micro-chips and dildo shaped remote-control devices. Many of them have backgrounds in the tech industry – Microsoft, NASA, AOL, Disney. They like to spend their leisure time playing with radio-controlled toys and gadgets, and the homes in Stepford are all installed with 'smart' features. For instance, Joanna and Walter's new house comes with a robotic pet dog, a refrigerator that monitors food stores, toilets that measure bodily functions and report on levels of blood sugar, protein and body fat, and a computerised security system that locks all the doors and windows at the touch of a button. The film's opening montage shows women celebrating the latest 1950s domestic technology, but as Friedan points out, rather than liberating women from the slog of housework, these innovations paradoxically create more work, functioning to further yoke housewives to domestic chores (Friedan, 1963, pp.233-57). It is perhaps no coincidence then that the technology in Oz's *Stepford* works against the women too. The smart features of Joanna's home do not just surveil her, they entrap her. After Bobby and Rodger turn into 'zombies,' Joanna announces to Walter that she is going to take the children and leave Stepford. However, she is unable to unlock the door. She presses the wrong buttons on the security panel and must rely on Walter to enter the proper code and let her out. The Stepford wives are not just ensnared by the machinations of the Female Improvement System; technology works against them on every level.

Paradoxically, as Susanne Leonard identifies, while the original *Stepford Wives* imagines technology as hostile to women's 'essential' nature, the remake accuses women of turning themselves into robots without the help of men (2009, p.17). After being exposed, Claire proclaims: 'I decided to turn back the clock: to a time before overtime, before quality time, before women were turning themselves into robots.' This admission makes no sense in the context of the automating procedures imposed on the women after their arrival in Stepford, which is confusing in itself. On the one hand the wives are revealed to be trans-human, technologically modified versions of their original selves – not androids. But earlier scenes clearly depict the wives as robots. One even doubles as an automatic teller machine, dispensing cash out of her mouth.

In contrast, Forbes' film unambiguously takes the time to juxtapose Joanna's natural body with various manufactured figures – not only her own replica, but the bodies of the other robot wives and the store mannequin shown in the opening sequence. Leonard makes the important point that Forbes is especially conscious of representations of the female body (2009, p.17). Binary oppositions of natural/ unnatural, organic/synthetic are continually juxtaposed through *mise en scène*. Joanna is predominantly filmed outdoors in fields and gardens and most of her photography takes place in nature, beyond the artificiality of the town of Stepford. A great deal of attention is given to Joanne and Bobbie's natural bodies, which they comfortably reveal through minimalistic clothing and the absence of restricted, structured items like bras. In stark contrast, the artificial wives' bodies are restricted and covered with layers of fabric – corsets, floor length skirts, aprons, high necklines. When Joanna is confronted with her replacement, the camera focuses on the obviously artificial, and significantly larger, breasts of the robot. As Leonard suggests, masculine technologies in the film are hostile to women's essential nature. The attention given to Joanna's natural breasts 'underscores femininity as an essentialised category, one that will soon be corrupted and forcefully taken over by technologies designed to interfere with the female body's biological functioning and inclinations' (2009, p.17). However, in the postfeminist remake, this critique becomes lost in a minefield of inexplicable contradictions.

Though a great deal of the film's ambiguity is indicative of postfeminism, this is compounded by issues with the making of the film itself. As revealed in this chapter's opening quote, Oz himself considers the film a mess, and it is easy to agree. For Oz, the main issue was that he went against his instincts, which were calling for 'something intimate.' Instead the movie became so big that his intuitions became lost (Merrick, *Ain't It Cool News*, 2007). According to Nancy Griffin, writing for *The New York Times* (2004), the remake was clearly a troubled project. Editing and the shooting of new scenes were continuing until just weeks before the film's release, and unusually, the producers, stars, and Oz did not make themselves available for promotional interviews.

Unlike the original *Stepford Wives*, which had a clear agenda (albeit one that was misinterpreted by some), the *Stepford Wives* remake cannot make up its mind what it is articulating. As Matrix argues, it can be seen as an expression of masculinity in crisis (2007, pp.109-19). It is brutally scathing of high-achieving career women, ridiculing and caricaturing them at any given opportunity. But equally, it is deeply disdainful of men, who are depicted as unattractive, nerdy misogynists. When King asks: 'What about all these other husbands [excluding Walter], are they still angry? Do they still want all these women to be robots?' Bobby replies: 'Of course! Men are pigs, they're disgusting, they're frightened repulsive little rodents.' The closing sequence of the film shows the Stepford husbands under house arrest in the supermarket where they are ordered to keep shopping. On one level, the film fetishises technology with its focus on gadgetry like the robo-puppy, but it is also scathing of rampant consumerism, especially 'boys' toys.' It articulates techno-anxiety about the potential misuse and abuse of technology as exemplified by Claire's megalomania and the way she manipulates innovations to satisfy her own selfish desires. Though part of the ambiguity of the film can be attributed to the conditions under which it was made, as Oz concedes, the remake is a posterchild for postfeminist discourses and ideologies that were especially prevalent around the early 2000s. Therefore, despite its numerous flaws, the remake offers important commentary about the social and cultural climate at the time of its creation – just as its predecessor does. It also loosely weaves in commentary about emerging directions in social robotics ubiquitous computing – the focus of the next and final chapter.

Chapter 7: Stepford Wives in the Real World

Caleb (Domhnall Gleeson): 'Why did you give her sexuality? An AI doesn't need a gender. She could have been a grey box.'

Nathan (Oscar Issac): 'Hmm. Actually, I don't think that's true. Can you give an example of consciousness, at any level, human or animal, that exists without a sexual dimension?' (*Ex Machina*, Garland, 2015)

'One in 10 young adults will have had sex with a humanoid robot by 2045.' (FutureofSex.net, 2020)

Jean Baudrillard describes sci-fi as an 'extravagant projection of real world production' (1991, pp.309-10). In other words, sci-fi is grounded in actuality, taking what is possible as inspiration to create plausible, yet simultaneously impossible worlds. Conversely, speculative story-bound imaginings operate as a means of scrutinizing and testing the complex dynamics between future innovation and society's responses to such modernizations. In doing so, fantastic worlds can shape the direction of technological development. Hence, it would be fair to claim that science and science fiction have a symbiotic relationship, each stimulating the other. Arguably, nowhere is this more evident than in relation to the development of social robots and other domestic AI technologies. Social robots are distinct from industrial and military automations in that they are intended to be comprehensively integrated into everyday life. It is anticipated that they will become increasingly useful for a variety of interpersonal tasks, particularly those related to human assistance and companionship. However, while social robots come in many forms, the type of machines presently receiving the vast majority of media attention are those constructed to look like hyper-sexualised women, as well as high-end sex dolls with integrated AI. In short, the wives of Stepford, while once purely a manifestation of long held imaginings about artificial women, are now a reality.

The purpose of this chapter is to explore the legacy of *The Stepford Wives* and the *Stepford* universe by examining real world directions in the development of AI sex dolls, social robots, and other gendered technologies. The chapter will scrutinise the social implications of deep machine learning and human-machine intimacy more broadly, particularly in the context of ubiquitous computing. It will question how progressively seamless interactions between humans, hardware and software will influence perceptions of intimacy with robots and AI in the future from a posthuman perspective. Finally, the chapter will investigate contemporary imaginings about android women on screen, focusing primarily on *Ex Machina*, which offers a modern re-imagining of the classic gothic trope of the self-aggrandised mad scientist with a god-complex. Of significance is a shift in character representation towards the subjective experiences of robot women themselves. This is also evident in other productions such as the series *Westworld*, *Humans*, and *Äkta Människor*.

Sex Dolls and Sex Robots

The dildo has existed since antiquity, originally as a ceremonial artefact and later as a medical aid for 'hysterical' women (Ferguson, 2014, p.15; van Driel, 2012, pp.65-9), but the sex doll has a more ambiguous past enmeshed with histories of other human replicas like conventional dolls, dummies, and automata. According to Anthony Ferguson in his book *The Sex Doll* (2014), the most direct antecedent of the modern sex doll has naval origins (2012, p.16). Evidently, it was common for seventeenth-century French and Spanish sailors to bring rudimentary life sized figurines known as *dames de voyage* or *dama de viaje* on long expeditions. However, it is not clear what these early 'ladies of the journey' might have looked like or how sophisticated they would have been since no specimens survive today. This is probably just as well since, as Ferguson points out, ships conditions were cramped, so one doll was likely shared among several men, rendering them a breeding ground for disease (2012, p.16).[18]

More tangible details about sex dolls can be traced to Irwin Bloch's 1909 book *The Sexual Life of Our Time*. Here Bloch, a medical doctor, details a whole range of sexual practices including necrophilia (which can be performed literally or symbolically through role play) and *Venus Statuaria*, which he describes as 'the love for and sexual intercourse with statues and other representations of the human person' (1909, p.648). He proposes that a taste for 'fornicatory dolls' finds origin in these two predilections. According to Bloch:

> There exists true Vaucansons in this province of pornographic technology, clever mechanics who, from rubber and other plastic materials prepare entire male or female bodies which, as *hommes* or *dames de voyage*, subverse fornicatory purposes. More especially are the genital organs represented in a manner true to nature. Even secretion of Bartholin's glands is imitated, by means of a 'pneumatic tube' filled with oil. Similarly, by means of fluid and suitable apparatus, the ejaculation of semen is imitated. Such artificial beings are actually offered for sale in the catalogue of certain manufacturers of 'Parisian Rubber Articles'. (Bloch, 1909, p.648)

Bloch (1909, p.649) also makes reference to Rene Schwaeblé's 1904 book *Les Détraqués de Paris* (*The Misfits of Paris*, pp.247-53), where a more precise account of fornicatory dolls is provided.[19] He further mentions the pornographic romance *La Femme Endormie* (*The Benumbed Woman*) published in Paris in 1899 by Madame B. The story focuses on a wealthy middle-aged man who, dissatisfied with real women, pays an artist a large sum of money to craft a perfect sex doll. As Jon Stratton (1996, p.213) points out, the story was clearly inspired by *L'Eve Future* (discussed in Chapter 2), except with an explicitly erotic focus.

There are unsubstantiated claims that the first modern sex doll was created by the Nazis under Heinrich Himmler, who was allegedly concerned about German troops contracting sexually transmitted diseases from foreign sex workers of 'inferior races.' His solution was the 'Model Borghild Project' – a special task force of experts appointed to design realistic, anatomically enticing, Aryan looking sex dolls to be transported with the troops across the European battlefields as tempting and acceptable alternatives to real women. However, the project was supposedly put on hold due to budget constraints following Germany's deepening commitment to global conquest. There is little evidence that the Borghild Project actually existed, aside from two photographs, which were later shown to be fake. Hence, the venture has since been dismissed as an elaborate hoax (Ferguson, 2012, pp.24-6).

What the Germans *did* make was the *Bild Lilli* doll: an 11.5 inch plastic pornographic figurine that was later replicated, re-branded, and patented as the wholesome, all-American Barbie doll by Mattel after the company's co-founder Ruth Handler discovered the figurines while travelling in Austria. M. G. Lord, describes the *Bild Lilli* doll as a lascivious plaything for adult men that was based on a comic character in the *Bild Zeitung*, a tabloid German newspaper (1994, p.7). Designed in 1955 by Max Weissbrodt, Lilli was an erotic caricature and Teutonic fantasy that came with a variety of seductive outfits. She could be positioned in provocative poses and was often placed on car dashboards and used as a sexual joke – though her ice-blond hair, pixie nose and shapely figure also make a strong statement about Aryan ideals. The original comic character Lilli – created by cartoonist Reinhard Beuthien – was a gold-digger and exhibitionist who used her looks to seduce and exploit sex-crazed business men. Beuthien's misogynistic jokes usually hinged on Lilli taking money from men and involved situations where Lilli wore very few clothes. In one cartoon, Lilly appears in a female friend's apartment, concealing her naked body with newspaper. The caption reading: 'We had a fight and he took back all the presents he gave me' (Lord, 1994, p.26). Another cartoon shows Lilli, costumed in a fitted black dress, talking with a female friend. The caption: 'How do you mean to marry a man with a lot of money? As soon as you marry him it will be gone' (Lord, 1994, p. 26).

However, while the *Bild Lilli* doll may have been pornographic, it does not fit with dominant understandings of a sex doll as a penetrable object. Inflatable, 'blow-up' dolls are the first modern incarnations of the fully interactive sex doll. Originating in Europe, the inflatable doll became popular in the 1960s and 1970s as a sex aid and novelty item that could be purchased under the counter at select adult bookstores. It is cheaply made from vinyl plastic with a painted on face and hair and it is prone to splitting at the seams if too much weight is placed on it (Ferguson, 2012, p.30). Mid-range dolls made of latex are sturdier and have more realistic features and body parts, but it is high-end, silicone dolls that this chapter is interested in. These products are state-of-the-art, with increasing verisimilitude to actual humans. The domestic availability of the internet has proven vital to marketing and dissemination of sex dolls, particularly in regard to buyer anonymity, and there has been a growing demand for them. The web is also a furtive site for sex doll databases, forums, and pornography sites, some of which specialise in sex doll porn only, along with others that offer sex doll porn videos as a sub-category of other fetishes.

There are a number of companies that make high-end sex dolls. These can be ordered online and shipped straight to the customer's door. For instance, the North Carolina company 1st PC sells the 'Natalie Doll' – a stock model made from thermoplastic polymer with a steel skeleton. Natalie comes with a brunette wig, three sets of interchangeable eyes (brown, blue, and green), and a hand held USB heater to warm openings. This model is fairly basic; especially in comparison to the products available at Tokyo based Orient Industries who claim to have been making sex dolls since 1977. Their website Orient Doll offers a wide selection of life-like sex mannequins each with various options including body (specifically breast) shape, head type, skin colour (normal, white, and suntanned), and hair style. Similarly, Californian Company Abyss Creations, which has specialised in high-end, anatomically correct, silicone sex-dolls (called RealDolls) for over twenty years, offers the ability to customize products from an extensive array of interchangeable (replaceable) parts, including faces, eyes, and labia. RealDolls are made primarily out of silicone with an articulated skeleton and come in a range of heights from 4 foot 10 inches to 5 foot 10 inches, as well as an extensive variety of eye, hair, and skin colours. More recently, their newly formed 'Realbotix' division has begun developing a range of sex robots. Some of the technologies available in these automated RealDolls include synchronization with an Android OS Application to facilitate the live streaming of 'spontaneous' conversation, personality trait options, inbuilt cameras for facial recognition of the doll's owner, memory capabilities (for recalling names and other personal details), facial animation, internal core-heating (replicating live human body temperatures) and sensor technology enabling the doll to simulate sexual responses, including the release of lubrication and spasmodic tightening of penetrative cavities.[20]

US Company TrueCompanion boasts the world's first sex robot: Roxxxy (Version 9). Unlike RealDolls, Roxxxy has only one physical option (or two if her soon to be released male counterpart Rocky is taken into account), but Roxxxy does have interchangeable personalities. Using a machine learning algorithm called 'Foundational AI', the company promotes the sex doll's ability to talk, listen, and conduct a conversation. Reportedly, the Foundational AI adapts to the owner's personality to give the impression of shared interests, but Roxxxy also comes with a variety of preconfigured 'personalities': 'Wild Wendy', 'Mature Martha', 'S&M Susan',

'Frigid Farah', and 'Young Yoko'. The conversational language interface can also operate off-line, independently from the internet (though presumably, preliminary downloads and software updates require connectivity). Available YouTube videos of a person called 'Dr Oz' having a discussion with Roxxxy do reveal the machine to have a natural sounding voice and seemingly spontaneous responses to questions that legitimize the company's claims about their product's conversational abilities.[21]

The larger robotics industry too has a strong interest in creating human-like machines, many of which are designed to look like hyper-feminised women. Some examples include fashion model HRP-4C, constructed by the National Institute of Advanced Industrial Science and Technology (Tokyo, Japan); Kokoro's Actroid-DER series, which can be hired out as booth bunnies, fashion models, and hosts, among other things; and a Scarlett Johansson replica built by private Hong Kong citizen Ricky Ma. Hiroshi Ishiguro Laboratories (Osaka, Japan) also have a range of incredibly life-like robots, one of which – Geminoid F – starred in Kōji Kukada's 2015 film *Sayônara*, about a terminally ill woman (Bryerly Long) who inhabits a nuclear ravaged near-future Japan with an android as her only companion.

According to the 'Future of Sex Report'[22] authored by Jenna Owsianik and Ross Dawson, impending developments relevant to sex robot technology include advanced deep machine learning like IBM's Watson and Hanson Robotics' BINA48 – a humanoid robot modeled on a real person – Bina Aspen. BINA48's complex AI is compiled from extensive recordings of Aspen's personal beliefs, memories, attitudes, commentary, and mannerisms. From this foundational information, BINA48 became the first robot to enroll in and successfully complete a university course (in philosophy at Notre Dame de Namur University in California).[23] BINA48 fits with what Katherine Hayles describes as Artificial Life (AL): a form of complex AI that evolves machine learning /intelligence through pathways replicating the biological neural networking of the human brain (Hayles, 1999, p.238). The data input techniques used to build BINA48's AI bear eerie resemblance to *The Stepford Wives*, where Joanna and the other women of Stepford are asked to tape-record extensive lists of words, syllables, and other personal information, which are then used to simulate their 'personalities' in their machine doppelgängers once they are dead.

Applied to real life sex robots, AI and AL technologies will facilitate increasingly sophisticated interpersonal capabilities. The Future of Sex Report speculates that interactive sex toys equipped with sensors will be soon be used as the genitals for sex robots, meaning that these machines will collect intimate data, enabling them to continually adapt and upgrade their sexual skills in accordance with what their human users like the most. Indeed, albeit at the expense of privacy, there may come a time when having sex with a robot is more enjoyable than engaging intimately with another human, propelling age-old techno-sexual fantasies into reality. As AI theorist David Levy argues, in the future, it will become increasingly common place for humans to use robots for sex and moreover, to develop deep emotional attachments to them, radically transforming our ideas about what constitutes sexual identity and authentic love (Levy, 2009, p.22).[24]

It must be noted that developments in the sex-robot industry have been met with considerable backlash. Campaigns against sex robots maintain that high-end sex dolls and sex robots perpetuate gender inequality and the objectification of women through the power relations that are embedded in the production, design, and use of sex-dolls, which are foremost made by men, for men.[25] In her research on the Japanese robot industry, anthropologist Jennifer Robertson concludes that the field exemplifies 'retro-tech,' otherwise described as 'advanced technology in the service of traditionalism' (2010, p.28). According to Robertson, most Japanese roboticists reinforce, through their machines, unprogressive notions of gender dynamics and the sexual division of labor. Hence, while these developers are visionaries of technology, they are not necessarily imaginers of fresh or progressive cultural configurations and social arrangements. Retro-tech has parallels with what Imelda Whelehan describes as 'retro-sexism;' a term she uses to critique the way that, in postfeminist media culture, sexism is reframed and represented as quaintly nostalgic (Whelehan, 2000, pp.24-5). One example of this is the constant re-runs of misogynistic shows like *M*A*S*H* (CBS, 1972–1983) on free-to-air television. This, in turn, operates as a way of undermining the gains of feminism – a strategy that is intrinsic to postfeminist logic. As McRobbie argues, postfeminist discourses effectively operate to 'undo' feminism by drawing on and evoking feminism to suggest that it has been achieved and thus, no longer something to be concerned about (McRobbie, 2009, pp.11-12).

The dismantling and de-politicization of feminist concerns, in turn, provides space for retro-sexist discourses to flourish.

Heterotopias, Ubiquitous Computing, and the Posthuman

Despite the opposition, further development of hyper-realistic sex-robots and other sexual technologies is inevitable as long as there is a market for them. In fact, as interactions between humans, hardware, and software become progressively seamless and unobtrusive, the hybridised spaces created by ubiquitous computing (also referred to as ambient intelligence), coupled with perpetual connectivity, will more likely promote and naturalise intimate experiences between humans and machines. The partial disembodiment of humans in technologically mediated spaces, coupled with the partial embodiment of electronic interfaces and devices will increasingly generate counter-sites that exist between the real and imaginary – other spaces that align with what Foucault calls heterotopias. Foucault describes heterotopias as liminal 'places between places' (1986, p.24): 'other' locations that exist in contradiction to 'normal' spaces. While Foucault mainly focuses on material examples that have a precise function in society – prisons, psychiatric hospitals, cemeteries, city gardens, and ships – he also examines heterotopias in relation to utopias, which are sites with no real place. Specifically, he contemplates the mirror as both a utopia and heterotopia (1986, p.24). The reflection in the mirror is a utopia since it is a placeless location: In the mirror, one sees oneself over there, where one is not. The reflection does not exist in reality. But from the standpoint of the mirror, one is absent from where one actually is, instead appearing in the virtual space on the other side of the glass. According to Foucault, the mirror functions as a heterotopia because 'it makes this place that I occupy at the moment when I look at myself in the glass absolutely real, connected with all the space that surrounds it, and absolutely unreal, since in order to be perceived it has to pass through this vital point which is over there' (1986, p.24).

The concept of a mirror as a heterotopia can be extended to immersive virtual worlds, especially those experienced using 3D stereoscopic technologies. Here, one enters a utopic place where one is not, but it is also a place where one is – the digital interface operating as the point of interconnection, much like the mirror in Foucault's example. Once in an immersive VR space, the user can disconnect from their material location and enter an immaterial universe. But while VR puts people inside a computer-generated world, ubiquitous computing forces computers to live out in the environment with people, creating hybridised nomadic places. Hence, in contrast to VR environments, where one can move around without changing one's physical position, nomadic technologies move through physical spaces with us via devices that are continually connected to the internet – smart watches and other wearables, smart phones, and tablets, along with the applications downloaded onto them are all examples of nomadic technologies. Home operating systems, hologram companions like Hikari Azuma, smart televisions and fridges are less mobile, but nonetheless ubiquitous and ambient, silently communicating with each other and collecting data that is transmitted and received via the internet. Through continual infiltration of the internet of things into the everyday, the notion of place/space becomes fragmented and destabilised, creating heterotopic 'places between places' everywhere – ubiquitous heterotopias if you will.

This is the primary aim of ubiquitous computing – to be pervasive, embedded, nomadic, and adaptable, as the vision statement for MIT's Project Oxygen: Pervasive, Human-Centred Computing makes clear:

> In the future, computation will be human-centred. It will be freely available everywhere, like batteries and power sockets, or oxygen in the air we breathe. It will enter the human world, handling our goals and needs and helping us to do more while doing less. We will not need to carry our own devices around with us. Instead, configurable generic devices, either handheld or embedded in the environment, will bring computation to us, whenever we need it and wherever we might be. As we interact with these 'anonymous' devices, they will adopt our information personalities. They will respect our desires for privacy and security. We won't have to type, click, or learn new computer jargon. Instead, we'll communicate naturally, using speech and gestures that describe our intent ('send this to Hari' or 'print that picture on the nearest colour printer'), and leave it to the computer to carry out our will.[26]

Ideas articulated by Project Oxygen find their origin in the theoretical work of computer scientist Mark Weiser. In his 1993 paper 'Ubiquitous Computing,' Weiser predicts a future where PCs will be obsolete. Instead, computer access will be all over the place – in walls, on our wrists, and in scrap computers, like unused paper, lying about as needed (1993, p.71). Importantly, this computing will take place in the background, leaving people feeling as though they did things themselves, seamlessly integrated into the environment, enhancing everyday activities (Weiser, 1993, p.71). Currently, humans are increasingly tied to their devices, but in the future, technologies such as personal bots take over many activities for us.

The idea of a time when the human body is seamlessly articulated with intelligent machines aligns with critical discourses about posthumanism. Posthumanism is an ambivalent and highly contested term, but fundamentally, it is a school of thought that arises from an interrogation of the status of the body and the self in relation to technology, calling into question persistent binaries such as self/other, organic/synthetic, culture/nature, mind/body, maker/made – dualisms that for prominent thinker Donna Haraway are systemic to the logics and practices of social and political domination (1987, p.93). As Katherine Hayles argues: 'In the posthuman, there are no essential differences or absolute demarcations between bodily existence and computer simulation, cybernetic mechanism and biological organism, robot technology and human goals' (Hayles, 1999, p.3). Importantly, for Hayles, the 'post' in posthuman signifies a continuum of human existence and change. Under this definition, posthumanism becomes part of the process of being human, which involves shaping and being shaped by our environments. Ideas about the body and embodiment (the sense that we occupy our bodies rather than merely possess them) are not static; they shift as cultures and the environment change. Citing Hayles again: 'Living in a technologically engineered and information-rich environment brings with it associated shifts in habits, postures, enactments, perceptions – in short, changes in the experiences that constitute the dynamic lifeworld we inhabit as embodied creatures' (Hayles, 2002, p.299).

Body boundaries have fluidity. When we extend our body and our bodies capabilities through technology, we are also expanding our body's schema and the flow of information. One can feel technologies as unconscious extensions of the body;

for instance, the symbiotic relationship between a gamer and their controller or a motorbike rider and their machine. These intersections alter the structure of the brain through the formation of new neurological pathways and connections. This in turn shapes the central and peripheral nervous system so that over time, through history, humans have become radically different. Hayles also challenges human-centric ways of thinking about the body as separate from the world – of our skin as some kind of limit of ourselves: a view that ignores the fact that the body is pierced with a myriad of openings that admit the environment. Particle matters are sucked in through our lungs, gasses are converted, viruses travel in our blood vessels and bacteria form their own microbiomes in our gastrointestinal tracts. The body enfolds the world and the world enfolds the body, causing the notion of the skin as a boundary to fall apart (Hayles, 2002, p.311). This complicates the idea of a human essence and of nature as a distinct category.

Two other elements encompassing the posthuman which disrupt essentialist, binary notions about humans and their interrelationship with technology, nature, and non-human animals are that, firstly, embodiment in a biological substrate is an accident of history rather than an inevitability of life. This implies that embodiment is not necessarily anchored to an organic form, but that potentially, it can exist beyond this. Secondly, that consciousness is an epiphenomenon – a by-product of brain activity rather than the seat of humanity as it is commonly conceived in western traditions (Hayles, 1999, pp.2-3). These aspects of posthumanist theory are increasingly relevant in the context of directions in AI and AL. Not only are humans becoming ever more enmeshed with technology, but technologies are becoming progressively more human-like – advances in complex neural machine learning being just one example. High-tech culture heightens human connections to their technologies, making fundamental ontological separation between organic and synthetic increasingly impossible to distinguish. As Haraway maintains, 'it is not clear who makes and who is made in the relation between human and machine. It is not clear what is mind and what body in machines that resolve into coding practice. In so far as we know ourselves in both formal discourse (for example, biology) and in daily practice [...] we find ourselves to be cyborgs, hybrids, mosaics, chimeras' (Haraway, 1987, p.93).

Female Androids on Screen in an Age of Deep Machine Learning

Realities concerning machine cognition introduce philosophical and ethical questions about awareness and subjectivity: At what point does the difference between robots/AI simulating emotion and them having actual feelings become a moot point? If consciousness is an epiphenomenon, can machines experience it in a similar way to organic species? If so, will there be a need for legislation protecting robot rights in the future? Will AI leave human intelligence redundant? If this is the case, what augmentations will humans require to compensate for this? These questions and others relating to machine sentience have led to some significant shifts, not only in relation to the way people imagine real-world interactions with intelligent technologies, but also in fictional representations of androids and AI in recent film and television texts – particularly female AI. As has been established in Chapter 2, imaginings about female androids have historically involved reducing women to their most manageable and objectified form – as occurs in *The Stepford Wives*. This trope is grounded in patriarchal anxiety about both the feminine and technology where the two become conflated as a common signifier of Otherness. In psychoanalytic terms, these patriarchal tensions manifest in the sadistic urge to control and dominate that which is relegated to the position of the Other. As has been established, *The Stepford Wives* is about Joanna's subjective experiences as a woman, but her robot replacement is no more than a contraption.

However, since the early 2010s, there has been an increasing number of sci-fi films and television productions that locate android women as complex characters, often examining the subjective point-of-view of the machine itself. Furthermore, the female robots in these texts are active, independently thinking, and consequently often fed up with being objectified and misused. *Ex Machina*, *Westworld*, *Humans*, and *Äkta Människor* all feature android women that are framed this way. Representations of female gendered machines in each of these texts disrupt masculine–active, feminine–passive binaries that have overwhelmingly existed in stories about men who create artificial women. Drawing on the work of Gilles Deleuze, who revises Freud's theory of masochism by positioning it in the pre-oedipal stage of development (instead of the oedipal phase as proposed by Freud, 1919), film scholar Gaylyn Studlar suggests that the masochist does not desire to sadistically control or destroy women, but rather to idealise them, submit to them, and be punished by them (1990, pp.229-49).

This shift from sadistic urges to control and destroy women, to masochistic fantasies about being usurped by them can be seen, in the context of imaginings about female robots, as a contemporary response to both high-tech culture and to current manifestations of gender politics in media. As Gill argues, 'feminism has a visibility in media culture that it did not have even a few years ago, and we are currently witnessing a resurge of feminist discourse and activism as well as a renewed interest in feminist stories' (2016, p.615). This form of 'popular feminism,' as it is described by Sarah Banet-Weiser (2018), differs on a surface level to postfeminism in that it is highly visible and concerned with the vast gender inequalities that continue to exist culturally, politically, and economically, shifting away from the ambivalence that characterizes postfeminism (Banet-Weiser, 2018). Hence, though it is grounded in the same neoliberal ideologies as postfeminism, it is far more pessimistic about gender equality, leading to some significant shifts in female representations in fiction. This includes an increased visibility of active, assertive, retribution-focused women in many genres, including sci-fi.

Masochistic articulations of technophobia align the female robot with techno-paranoiac tropes typically attached to male gendered machines in film fiction: a form of techno-imagining akin to that articulated in Capek's R.U.R. One prominent example is The Gunslinger in Crichton's original *Westworld*. The Gunslinger is built to be 'killed,' repeatedly, by patrons at the Westworld amusement park. However, following an unexplained computer glitch, human-robot power dynamics are reversed. The technical error transforms The Gunslinger into an unrelenting, out-of-control death machine that systematically annihilates the humans who have previously taken great pleasure in destroying him. In the television series *Westworld*, 'host' Dolores (Evan Rachel Wood) becomes a female gendered equivalent to The Gunslinger after an unexplained update malfunction leads to a conscious awakening. Both Dolores and fellow host Maeve (Thandiwe Newton) begin to form cohesive memories of the repeated rape, abuse, and murder inflicted on them for decades by various visitors. As they undergo this transformation, so too is the viewer aligned with their experiences. This positioning reconfigures the female robot, shifting the narrative focus to the character as a complex subject rather than a one-dimensional object and by-product of male megalomania as is the case in *The Stepford Wives*.

Television's *Westworld* knowingly speaks back to posthuman understanding of consciousness as an epiphenomenon. For instance, when the park's creator Robert Ford (Anthony Hopkins) as confronted with questions about machine sentience he asserts:

> There is no threshold that makes us greater than our sum of parts, no inflection point at which we become fully alive. We can't define consciousness because consciousness does not exist. Humans fancy that there is something special about the way we perceive the world, and yet we live in loops as tight and closed as the Hosts do, seldom questioning our choices. ("Trace Decay" Season 1, Episode 8)

A prime example of this is the 'Man in Black' (Ed Harris), who is compelled to return to Westworld over and over, brutalising, raping, and murdering Dolores each time he visits. The Man in Black is later revealed to be a much older version of a man called William (Jimmi Simpson), who initially fell in love with Dolores on his first visit to the park many years earlier before realising that her seemingly conscious state and genuine emotions were in fact a part her programmed response to all guests.

Ex Machina deploys archetypal gothic narrative conventions of the self-aggrandised 'mad scientist' in order to present a powerful critique of masculine cultures of technology and the social assumptions about sex difference that are entrenched within it. The film destabilises traditional tropes of artificial women in fiction by locating the two central female robot characters as calculating, rebellious, and of far superior intellect than the man who crafted them. Principal to *Ex Machina* is a remarkably engineered robot named Ava (Alicia Vikander). Ava is built by reclusive billionaire genius/madman Nathan Bateman, CEO of the technology company 'Blue Book' (a fictional equivalent of Google).[27] The film opens with Caleb, a young computer programmer employed by Blue Book, winning a 'lottery' competition to spend a week with Nathan in his remote Alaskan estate, which doubles as a state-of-the-art research facility. After signing a less than standard non-disclosure agreement, Nathan reveals that the reason Caleb is there, is to be the human component in a contemporary version of the 'Turing Test': the colloquial name for an experiment devised in 1950 by computer scientist Alan Turing as a way of addressing the possibility of machine cognition. Turing's test relies on indirect communication with a hidden computer and its ability to fool a human subject into thinking they are interacting with a living person (Turing, 1950, pp.433-60). However, for Nathan, the real test is to show Caleb that Ava is a machine, and then see if he feels that she has a consciousness – that aside from her obvious artificiality, she is, for all intents and purposes, human, with (seemingly) authentic emotions. What Caleb does not realise is that Ava is based on his pornography profile and has been strategically programmed to seduce him using human-centric traits of imagination, self-awareness, empathy, sexuality, and manipulation – a 'true' measure of AI according to Nathan. What Caleb also does not know is that Ava is the latest in a long line of prototypes, including Nathan's mute servant/companion Kyoko (Sonoya Mizuno) – Ava's predecessor who has been stripped of her higher functions and reprogrammed to 'help around the house and be fucking awesome in bed.'

Like fictional mad scientists before him, including Dale Cobra and his cronies, Nathan does not just produce life without a mother; he creates woman herself, the epitome of nature (Huyssen, 1981, p.227). Hence, woman, nature, and machine are conflated into one object that is entirely subject to the whims of its egomaniacal inventor. Because Nathan gives rise to his sentient machines, he believes that he can do what he wants with them. This includes physically, sexually, and 'emotionally' abusing them, and decommissioning them on impulse. Nathan takes pride in the fact that his robots are anatomically complete with cavities that emulate vaginas, including concentrations of electro-sensors that operate like nerve endings, equipping his machines with 'pleasure response' capabilities. Hence, as obsessed as Nathan is with perfecting his human replicas, ultimately, they serve no higher purpose than sex objects for him, just like the robot wives of Stepford are for their husbands.

As self-aggrandised as Nathan is, he also exhibits nihilism and masochistic fatalism about his pursuits. He regularly drinks himself into a stupor, occasionally reciting slurred renditions of J. Robert Oppenheimer's despondent verses, written after he realized the gravitas of his role as head of The Manhattan Project. Often referred to as 'father of the atomic bomb,' Oppenheimer acknowledges: 'When you see something that is technically sweet, you go ahead and do it and you argue about what to do about it only after you have had your technical success' (Oppenheimer cited in Easley, 1983, p.129). When asked by Caleb why he made Ava (and her prototypes), Nathan's response is that strong AI technology is inevitable, that Ava is not a decision, she is evolution. In Nathan's fatalistic, but fundamentally narcissistic view, AI will eventually take over the world, rendering the human species extinct, just as nuclear weaponry has the potential to do. But the lure of achievement is too 'technically sweet' and so Nathan develops his state-of-the-art sex machines regardless.

In regard to philosophical questions about consciousness, emotions, and authenticity, it is suggested that the answer to this lies in Caleb's emotional responses to Ava. That it is *he* who provides legitimacy to the feelings that she emulates in order to manipulate him. This is reinforced by the fact that Caleb seemingly never queries the validity of Ava's reciprocal desire for him. Once Ava achieves her goal of escaping, she displays no regard for Caleb. Instead, she leaves him sealed in the in the research facility, alone with the carcasses of Nathan, Kyoko, and the other decommissioned machine women that came before her. The only authentic emotion that Ava does seem to possess is hatred of Nathan. As Riviere (1929) theorizes, femininity can be performed as a means of getting by in patriarchal society. In *L'Eve Future*, the notion of female performativity is used by Edison to justify building a replica Alicia (see Chapter 2). For him, women are so riddled with fakery in their natural state that creating an artificial version is really no different and infinitely beneficial, since there are no fleshly grotesqueries to deal with. In *The Stepford Wives*, the Stepford women's failure to perform idealized traditional femininity is used as a reason to replace them with versions that do. Conversely, in *Ex Machina*, performances of femininity are used by Ava as a façade – a ploy with which to seduce Caleb and escape (just as Nathan had programmed her to do).

This marks an important shift in character representation in sci-fi film and television. As established earlier in this chapter, Ava and contemporary female gendered androids like her are reimagined as sentient killers, much like many male robots in fiction. However, it would be wrong to simply locate them as mechanized *femmes fatale*. Ava is deadly, but she is also an avenger with a justified desire for retribution that extends beyond the limits of her programming, as is her sister-machine Kyoko. Likewise, Maeve and Dolores in *Westworld* have suffered decades of violence inflicted on them by men, making their desire for revenge wholly warranted. Cinematic depictions of rape-revenge first became popular in the early 1970s, although Ingmar Bergman's *The Virgin Spring* (1960) is considered a prototype (Alexander, 2005). Like gothic women's films discussed in Chapter 1, the rape-revenge narrative is typically presented from a woman's perspective and sees the protagonist seek retribution because she, her friend, or her relative has been raped and/or murdered by a male or group of males. Classic 1970s rape-revenge films include Wes Craven's *The Last House on the Left* (1972), Toshiya Fujita's *Lady Snowblood* (1973), Lemont Johnson's *Lipstick* (1976), and Meir Zarchi's *I Spit on Your Grave* (1978). Given the active, central role of women in these films, their refusal to tolerate male abuse, along with a common focus on actual or symbolic castration (such as stabbing), the rape-revenge film style can be interpreted as a both a feminist and a masochistic response to violence against women. With this in mind, it is not surprising that sci-fi productions featuring merciless female robots should emerge in an era of renewed focus on gender inequality and women's rights in popular media. As has been established throughout this book, creative works often function as a product of the socio-cultural climate of their creation, articulating anxieties relevant to the time. On the one hand, *Ex Machina* plays out established recurring themes about android women that find origin in *L'Eve Future*. Simultaneously, it subverts these misogynistic fantasies. Nathan may reduce his high-tech creations to little more than complex, yet disposable, sex toys, but unlike his predecessors – most notably the men of Stepford – in an age of popular feminism and machine intelligence, he cannot, and does not, get away with it.

This book has shown that fantasies about artificial women are historically entrenched. But importantly, they are not static. Instead, they are very much reflective of the socio-cultural, political, and technological climate at the time of their creation. Contemporary society is increasingly proliferated by ubiquitous computing where spaces and places are permeated by seamless interactions between humans, hardware and software, destabilising organic/synthetic binaries to create environments that are best described as ubiquitous heterotopias. These hybridised settings alter human-machine interactions on progressively intimate levels. The way

Gatebox's holographic Azuma Hikari is marketed as an ideal companion and 'bride' is just one example. Another is the demand for realistic sex-dolls with integrated AI. Significantly, this has prompted some radical shifts in sci-fi imaginings about artificial women focused on techno-paranoid ideas about the potential consequences of advanced AI and high-end sex dolls with machine sentience. In *The Stepford Wives* the robot women are the end-product of systemic misogyny, stripped of subjectivity and complexity. In recent film and television android women are themselves multifaceted, cognisant (fabricated) beings. Not only are they given subjectivity in the storyworlds they occupy, they are clearly unimpressed with the way they have been treated so far. They are the new avengers.

Concluding Comments

As has been noted in Chapter 7, contemporary productions like *Ex Machina* and *Westworld* mark a significant turning point in sci-fi representations of artificial women. Since industrialisation and early works such as *L'Eve Future*, female robots have functioned as a sadistic fantasy offering a solution to the 'problem' of the unruly organic women with their flaws and fakery. Hyussen suggests that fantasy's female robots originate in fears about industrialisation, when increasingly powerful machines began to be perceived as harbingers of chaos and destruction. The inexplicable threat of industrial capitalism is then recast and reconstructed in terms of male fear about female sexuality (1981, p.226). Certainly, though stories about artificial women date back to antiquity, it is not until industrialisation that clear patterns emerge where woman and machines are routinely conflated into a single automated object. Overwhelmingly, the fusion of women with machines has to do with the maintenance and stabilisation of patriarchal domination, where femininity is anchored to nature, and male mastery over technological innovation is deployed to secure power over both. As a result, sci-fi and science have cultivated an interdependent relationship. Imaginings about female androids have most certainly shaped conceptual ideas and developments in the field of social robotics and sex dolls, but in an age of complex AI and developments in deep machine learning, including machines like BINA48, it is increasingly necessary to conceive of a future where artificial women, including sex robots, will also be equipped with these technologies. For instance, Ava is depicted as an advanced piece of engineering much like Hadaly is in *L'Eve Future*, but her 'wetware' – an ellipse orb filled with structural gel containing thousands of neuron-like tendrils that can arrange and rearrange on a molecular level, enabling her to hold memory and shift thought – presents a new complexity to the figure of the artificial woman that is in keeping with real world theoretical models of artificial neural networks. This changes the fundamental nature of the android in fiction, relocating the machine woman as a multifaceted, cognisant character. It also represents an inevitable shift in representation, away from mollifying anxieties about the feminine by reducing it to its most basic, controllable form, towards masochistic, technophobic desires involving idealisation, submission, and punishment by powerful android women with beyond-human intelligence.

Moreover, fictional imaginings about artificial women are not only attached to science, they are also enmeshed with gender politics. Feminism is presently receiving visibility in media and popular culture that it did not have earlier in the millennium. There is a focus on demands for action regarding issues like sexism, domestic violence, and gender pay gaps, as well as a gradual recognition the intersectionality of women's experiences was ignored by earlier (hegemonic) feminisms. While these feminist visibilities are uneven, complicated, and grounded in neoliberalism, as scholars like Banet-Weiser (2018) and Gill (2010) have rightly noted, they have led to shifts in screen representations of women in genres like sci-fi, action, and horror. This includes a resurgence of themes of rape-revenge that find origin in second wave feminist activism of the 1960s and 1970s.[28]

As this book has shown through its extended analysis of *The Stepford Wives* and the *Stepford* universe, whenever feminism gains some form of traction, there are patriarchal reactions. It is an unlikely coincidence that fictional works such as *L'Eve Future* with its scathing assessment of the feminine form and obsessive desire to deconstruct womanliness, stripping it of its 'scaffolding' and ridding it of its intellectually and morally 'flawed' character, emerged at a time when women's rights, particularly suffrage, were gaining political and legislative headway. *The Stepford Wives* extends the fantasies enacted in *L'Eve Future*. Much like Edison and Lord Ewald before them, the husbands of Stepford take issue with their transgressive wives who have thoughts, opinions and interests outside the domestic sphere. They too want to assassinate the 'triumphant animal nature' of the women they have married, re-craft their bodies to their own specifications, and do so via the substitution of flesh for metal and other 'man-made' materials. Nonetheless, *The Stepford Wives* marks a radical transition in character representation. Like *Rosemary's Baby* before it, *The Stepford Wives* is not about men, it is about women trying to navigate a society at a time when patriarchal control over women's bodies is the norm and where dominant discourses dictate that women are second class citizens. The android wives of Stepford operate as allegory for what Freidan describes as the mystique of femininity – a principle grounded in post-World War II politics and the myth of the happy suburban housewife. The horror experienced by Joanna as she confronts the reality that her husband, along with the rest of the Men's Association, is planning to murder and replace her, metaphorically articulates Friedan's 'problem that has no name.' Thus, regardless of criticism levelled at *The Stepford Wives* by some critics and activists following the film's release, it charts an important point in the history of gender politics, albeit one dominated by liberal feminism and the challenges faced by a narrow sub-set of white, middle-class, heterosexual suburban women.

Likewise, other films in the Stepford canon are revealing of the socio-political climate at the time of their production. This is especially true for *The Stepford Husbands* and Oz's re-imagining of Forbes' film. *The Stepford Husbands* enacts Faludi's well-known backlash thesis with all the subtlety of a sledgehammer. The gender reversals at play in the film are scathing of ambitious women, particularly Dr Borzage, founder of the 'Stepford Clinic for Problem Men,' who is depicted as ruthless and self-serving. The drug treatment endured by the husbands and their overall lack of authority in the town leaves them seething with feelings of patriarchal impotence and rage; the implication being that not only is feminism a failed experiment, it is causing a crisis, and women's desire to have-it-all is to blame (Faludi, 1991, p.2). Oz's version of *The Stepford Wives* is more comprehensively imbued with postfeminist logic, enacting prominent tropes including the vilification of high-powered career women, retreatist fantasises, the romanticisation of traditionalism, and a time less complicated by gender politics. Joanna is reimagined as an overbearing, overambitious, 'career bitch' who people want to kill, and mad scientist Claire Wellington is a deranged murderer with a misplaced nostalgia for a time when women aspired to the mystique of femininity. This kind of narrative content is constitutional of postfeminism which involves an entanglement with feminism whereby it is taken into account yet simultaneously attacked (McRobbie, 2009, p.12). Oz's *Stepford Wives* marks a particular point in the history of female representation in popular culture where postfeminist discourses were articulated in predictable ways. This generated important insights at the time. However, gender politics has changed in recent years, at least on a surface level. It is debatable how transgressive these shifts are when considering current directions in social robotics. Not only is there a robust and expanding industry in high-end sex dolls with integrated AI, but social robots made for more general purposes like domestic help and the service industry are often gendered female and presented in traditional, hyper-sexualised ways. These depictions work to reinstall and revitalise retro-sexist myths about gender and sex difference, especially regarding the role of women in the domestic sphere and unskilled jobs. Hence, as Gill rightly cautions, feminism is certainly popular at the moment, marking a profound shift from dominant discourses circulating a decade ago, but this does not mean these changes are fixed and secure or that feminist politics are hegemonic (2010, p.619). This prompts questions about what future iterations of artificial women will look like.

REFERENCES

Abernethy, J. (1814) *An Enquiry into the Probability and Rationality of Mr. Hunter's Theory of Life*, London: Longman, Hurst, Rees, Orme, and Brown.

Alexander, J. R. (July-September, 2005) 'The Maturity of a Film Genre in an Era of Relaxing Standards of Obscenity: Takashi Ishii's *Freeze Me* as a Rape-Revenge Film', *Senses of Cinema* 36.

Avila E. (2005) 'Dark City: White Fright and the Urban Science Fiction Film in Postwar America', pp.88-97 in S. Redmond (ed.) *Liquid Metal: The Science Fiction Film Reader*, New York: Wallflower Press/Columbia University Press.

Banet-Weiser, S. (2018) 'Postfeminism and Popular Feminism', *Feminist Media Histories*.

Bartholomew, D. (1975) 'The Stepford Wives' *Cinefantastique* 4.2: 40-2.

Baudrillard, J. and A. B. Evans. (1991) 'Simulacra and Science Fiction', *Science Fiction Studies* 18.3: 309-313.

Beaudreau, A. and S. Finger. (2006) 'Medical Electricity and Madness in the 18th Century: The Legacies of Benjamin Franklin and Jan Ingenhousz' *Perspectives in Biology and Medicine* 49.3: 330-345.

Beaupre, L. (1972) 'Hits Few: Beasts of Burden: Analysis of 1971 Boom-Bust Biz,' *Variety*, November 29: 5.

Beckford, W. (1786) *Vathek: An Arabian Tale*, New York: James Miller.

Bedini, S. A. (2013) 'The Role of Automata in the History of Technology' *Technology and Culture* 5.1: 24-42.

Beuka, R. (2004) *SuburbiaNation: Reading Suburban Landscape in Twentieth Century American Film and Fiction*, London: Palgrave.

Bloch, I. (1909) *The Sexual Life of Our Time: In Its Relations to Modern Civilisation*, London: Rebman Ltd.

Boruzkowski, L. A. (1987) '*The Stepford Wives*: The Re-Created Woman.' *Jump Cut* 32: 16-19.

Boston Women's Health Book Collective. *Our Bodies, Ourselves*, 1973.

Boucher, J. (Summer 2003) 'Betty Friedan and the Radical Past of Liberal Feminism,' *New Politics* ix.3: 23.

Bradbury, R. (March 1949) 'Marionettes Inc.' in *Startling Stories*, US: Standard Magazines.

Braddon, E. (1862) *Lady Audley's Secret*, Leipzig: Bernhard Tauchnitz.

Butler, J. (1988) 'Performative Acts and gender Constitution: An Essay in Phenomenology and Feminist Theory' *Theatre Journal* 40.4: 519-31.

Carpenter, M. (1943) *Experiment Perilous*, Boston: Little, Brown, & Company.

Castle, T. (1995) *The Female Thermometer: Eighteenth Century Culture and the Invention of the Uncanny*, Oxford: Oxford University Press.

Chesler, P. (2005) *Women and Madness*, London: Palgrave.

Cohn, L. (1980) '10-Year Diary of Fast-Fade 'Indie' Pix: Risky for Thesps when Direting' *Variety* October 15:13.

Collins, W. (1860) *The Woman in White*, London: Arcturus Publishing Limited.

Cook, D. (2002) *Lost Illusions: American Cinema in the Shadow of Watergate and Vietnam 1970-1979*, Berkeley: University of California Press.

Dabakis, M. (1982) 'Gendered Labor: Norman Rockwell's Rosie the Riveter and the Discourses of Wartime Womanhood.' pp. 182-294 in B.Melosh (ed.) *Gender and American History Since 1880*, New York: Routledge.

"Danger Ahead! Valium: The Pill You Love Can Turn on You' *Vogue* 165.2 (February 1 1975): 152-3.

de Beauvoir, S. (2009) *The Second Sex*. Trans. C. Borde and S. Malovany-Chavallier. London: Vintage.

De l'Isle-Adam, V. (1982) *Tomorrows Eve*. Trans. R. M. Adams. Chicago: University of Illinois Press.

Del Rey, L. (1938) 'Helen O'Loy', *New York: Astounding Science Fiction*.

'Derek Hill to Show Bryan Forbes 'Wives'' *Variety* December 29, 1976: 30.

Dickson, E. J. "Sex Doll Brothels are now a Thing: What Will Happen to Real-Life Sex Workers? *Vox* November 26 2018.

Dijkstra, S. (1980) 'Simone de Beauvoir and Betty Friedan: The Politics of Omission', *Feminist Studies* 6.2: 290-303.

Doane, M. A. (2004) 'Technophilia: Technology, Representation and the Feminine' pp. 182-90 in S. Redmond (ed.) *Liquid Metal: The Science Fiction Film Reader*, New York: Wallflower Press/Columbia University Press.

Dow, B. J. (2006) 'The Traffic in Men and the Fatal Attraction of Postfeminist Masculinity' *Women's Studies in Communication* 29.1:113-131.

du Maurier, D. (1938) *Rebecca*, Boston: Little, Brown, and Company.

_____. (1965) *The Flight of the Falcon*, London: Gollancz.

Easlea, B. (1983) *Fathering the Unthinkable: Masculinity, Scientists, and the Nuclear Arms Race*, London: Pluto.

Ebert, R. (1975) *The Stepford Wives* (Review) January 1.

Elliott, J. (2008) 'Stepford USA: Second-Wave Feminism, Domestic Labour, and the Representation of National Time', *Cultural Critique* 70: 32-62.

Elsaesser, T. (2004) 'American Auteur Cinema: The Last – or First – Great Picture Show', pp.37-69 in T.Elsasser, A. Horworth, N. King (eds) *The Last Great Picture Show*, Amsterdam: Amsterdam University Press.

Ehrenreich, B. and Deirdre E. (2010) *Witches, Midwives, and Nurses: A History of Women Healers*, New York: Feminist Press.

Faludi, S. (1991) *Backlash: The Undeclared War Against Women*. London: Chatto & Windus.

Ferguson, A. (2010) *Sex Doll: A History*, Jefferson: McFarland.

Forbes, B. (1992) *A Divided Life: Memoirs*, London: William Heinemann.

Forrest, N. (2004) 'The Stepford Wives', *the f word*, July 20 July.

Foucault, M. and J. Miskowiec. (1986) 'Of Other Spaces', *Diacritics* 16.1: 22-27.

_____. (1965) *Madness and Civilisation: A History of Insanity on the Age of Reason*. Trans. R. Howard, New York: Pantheon.

Fox, M. (2006) 'Betty Friedan, Who Ignited Cause in 'Feminine Mystique,' Dies at 85' *The New York Times*.

Friedan, B. (1972) *The Feminine Mystique*, New York: Dell.

Friedman, L. D. (2007) *American Cinema of the 1970s: Themes and Variations*, New Jersey, Rutgers University Press.

Freud, S. (1919) 'The Uncanny.' pp. 217-256 *Standard Edition of the Complete Psychological Works of Sigmund Freud Vol. XVII: An Infantile Neurosis and Other Works*. London: Hogarth, 2001.

_____. (1919) 'A Child is Being Beaten' pp. 97-122, in P. Reiff (ed.) *Sex and the Psychology of Love*, New York: Simon & Schuster.

'Galvanic Miracles' (January 6 1803), *The Morning Post*, London.

Galyean, C. (2015) *Levittown: The Imperfect Rise of the American Suburbs* http://ushistoryscene.com/?s=Levittown

Gans, H. (May-June 1975) 'Stepford Wives Killing Off Women's Liberation' *Social Policy*: 59-60.

_____. (1982) *The Levittowners: Ways of Life and Politics in a New Suburban Community*, New York: Columbia University Press.

Gill, R. (2008) 'Culture and Subjectivity in Neoliberal Postfeminist Times', *Subjectivity* 25: 432-45.

_____. (2016) 'Post-Postfeminism?: New Feminist Visibilities in Postfeminist Times' *Feminist Media Studies* 16.4: 610-630.

Goldman, W. (1983) *Adventures in the Screen Trade: A Personal View of Hollywood and Screen Writers*, New York, Warner Books.

Gregory, D. (2001) *The Stepford Life*. US.

Griffin, N. (2004) 'Can This Film Be Fixed?' *The New York Times*, June 6.

Haraway, D. (1987) 'A Manifesto for Cyborgs: Science, Technology, and Socialist Feminism in the 1980s' *Australian Feminist Studies* 2.4: 1-42.

Haskell, M. (1975) 'The Stepford Mummies –Taking Plastic Measures' *The Village Voice* Feb 26: 65-66.

Hawkins, C. (2004) 'I Married a Misogynist From Outer Space: The Challenge of Being a Bride in 1950s Science Fiction Films', *Femspec: San Francisco* 5.1: 37.

Hayles, K. (1999) *How We became Posthuman: Virtual Bodies in Cybernetics, Literature, and Informatics*, Illinois: University of Chicago Press.

_____. (2002) 'Flesh and Metal: Reconfiguring the Mindbody in Virtual Environments,' *Configurations* 10.2: 297-320.

Hegel, G.W.F. (2018) *The Phenomenology of Spirit*. Trans M. Inwood, Oxford; Oxford University Press.

Helford, E. R. (2003) 'It's a Rip-off of the Women's Movement: Second-Wave Feminism and the Stepford Wives.' pp. 24-39, in S.A. Innes (ed.) *Disco Divas: Women and Popular Culture in the 1970s*, Pennsylvania, University Pennsylvania Press.

_____. (2006) 'The Stepford Wives and the Gaze', *Feminist Media Studies* 6.2: 145-56.

Hendershot, C. (1998) 'The Invaded Body: Paranoia and Radiation Anxiety in *Invaders From Mars*, *It Came From Outer Space*, and *Invasion of the Body Snatchers*.' *Extrapolation* 39.1: 26-39.

Henry, J. (Nov 1865) 'Miss Braddon' *Nation* 9: 593-5.

Herzberg, D. (2010) *Happy Pills in America: From Miltown to Prozac*, Baltimore: John Hopkins University Press.

Hoffmann, E.T.A. (1816; 1967) 'The Sandman', pp. 183-214, *The Best Tales of Hoffmann*. Trans. E. F. Bleier, New York: Dover Publications.

Hoffmann, E.T.A. (1814; 1967) 'The Automata', pp. 71-103, *The Best Tales of Hoffmann*. Trans. E. F. Bleier, New York: Dover Publications.

hooks, bell. (2000) *Feminist Theory: From Margin to Centre*, 2nd Edn. London: Pluto.

_____. (2014) *Ain't I A Woman: Black Women and Feminism*, New York: Routledge.

Horowitz, D. (1998) *Betty Friedan and the Making of The Feminine Mystique: The American Left, The Cold War, and Modern Feminism*. Amherst: University of Massachusetts Press.

Horwitz, A. V. (2020) *Between Sanity and Madness: Mental Illness from Ancient Greece to the Neuroscientific Era*, Oxford: Oxford University Press.

Huyssen, A. (1981) 'The Vamp and the Machine: Technology and Sexuality in Fritz Lang's Metropolis', *New German Critique* 24/25: 221-237.

James, H. (1865) 'Review of Mary Braddon's Aurora Floyd', *The Nation*.

Jackson, S. (1968) 'The Beautiful Stranger' pp. 58-65, in *Come Along With Me*, New York: Viking Press.

Jentsch, Ernst. (1906) 'On the Psychology of the Uncanny' pp. 216-228 in J. Collins and J. Jervis (eds) *Uncanny Modernity: Cultural Theories, Modern Anxieties*, London: Palgrave, 2008.

Johnston, J. and Cornelia S. (2011) 'An Analysis of the Technoscientific Imaginary in the Remake of The Stepford Wives' *Wide Screen* 3.1.

Jones, B. and J. Brown. (1968) *Toward a Female Liberation Movement Redstockings of the Women's Liberation Movement*, Gainesville, Florida.

Jurca, C. (2011) *The American Novel and the Rise of the Suburbs*, Cambridge: Cambridge University Press.

Kael, P. (1975) 'Male Revenge' *The New Yorker* February 24: 110-13.

Kakoudaki, D. (2014) *Anatomy of a Robot: Literature, Cinema and the Cultural Work of Artificial People*, New York, Rutgers.

Kang, M. (2011) *Sublime Dreams of Living Machines: The Automaton in the European Imagination*, Massachusetts: Harvard University Press.

Keats, J. (1956) *Crack in the Picture Window*, New York: Literary Licencing.

Kellett, E.E. (1901) *The Lady Automaton*, Pearson's Magazine.

Kerr, B. 'Are Sex-Doll Brothels the Wave of the Future?' *Rolling Stone* November 18, 2018.

King, N. (2004) 'The Last Good Time We Ever Had': Remembering the New Hollywood Cinema,' pp. 19-36 in T. Elsasser, A. Horworth, and N.King (eds) *The Last Great Picture Show*, Amsterdam: Amsterdam University Press.

Kirby's Wonderful and Eccentric Museum or Magazine of Remarkable Characters, (1803-1820), London: London House Yard, St Peters.

Klemesrud, J. (1975) 'Feminists Recoil at Film Designed to Relate to Them' *The New York Times*, Feb 26: 29.

Krugovoy S. A. (2002) 'The Cyborg Mystique: "The Stepford Wives" and Second Wave Feminism,' *Women's Studies Quarterly* 30.1-2: 60-76.

Krumm, P. (1999) 'The Island of Doctor Moreau, or the Case of Devolution' *Foundation* 75: 51-62.

Lasch, C. (1997) 'Women and the Common Life: Love, Marriage, and Feminism' (ed.) Elisabeth Lash-Quinn, New York: Norton.

Levin, I. (1954) *A Kiss Before Dying*, London: Constable & Robinson Ltd.

_____. (1967) *Rosemary's Baby*, London: Constable & Robinson Ltd.

_____. (1972) *The Stepford Wives*, New York: Random House.

_____. (1991) *Sliver*, New York: Bantam Dell Publishing.

_____. (2003) 'Stuck With Satan' New American Library Edition of *Rosemary's Baby*.

Leonard, S. (2009) 'The Science of Stepford: Technologies of Sexuality in a Postfeminist Age.' Pp. 14-25 in K. A. Ritenhoff and K. A. Herms (eds) *Sex and Sexuality in a Feminist World*, Cambridge: Cambridge Scholars.

Lewis, M. (1796) *The Monk: A Romance*, Dublin.

Levy, D. (2009) *Love and Sex with Robots: The Evolution of Human-Robot Relationships*, New York: Harper Collins.

Lindop, S. *Postfeminism and the Fatale Figure in Neo-Noir Cinema*, London: Palgrave, 2015.

_____. (2014) 'Carmilla, Camilla: The Influence of the Gothic on David Lynch's Mulholland Drive,' *Media Culture Journal* 17.4.

Locke, H. and S. Finger (2006) 'Gentleman's Magazine, the Advent of Electricity and Disorders of the Nervous System,' pp. 257-270 in H. Whitaker, C.U.M Smith, and S. Finger (eds) *Brain Mind and Medicine: Essays in Eighteenth-Century Neuroscience*, New York: Springer.

Lord, M.G. (2004) *Forever Barbie: The Unauthorised Biography of a Real Doll*, London: Bloomsbury.

MacArthur, S. (2015) *Gothic Science Fiction: 1818 to the Present*, London: Palgrave.

Mainari, P. (2000) 'The Politics of Housework' pp.163-78 in M. Plotter and L. Umanski (eds) *Making Sense of Women's Lives: An Introduction to Women's Studies*, Oxford: Rowman and Littlefield.

Mann, K. (2004) 'You're Next!: Postwar Hegemony Besieged in Invasion of the Body Snatchers' *Cinema Journal* 44.1: 49-68.

Matrix, S. E. (2007) 'Behind the Idyllic Façade, a Terrible Secret: Technologies of Gender and Discourses of Diplomacy in The Stepford Wives', *Storytelling* 6.2: 109-19.

McDonagh, M. (2004) 'The Exploitation Generation Or: How Marginal Movies Came in From the Cold,' pp. 107-130 in T. Elsasser, A. Horworth, and N.King (eds) *New Hollywood Cinema in the 1970s*, Amsterdam: Amsterdam University Press.

McRobbie, A. (2009) *The Aftermath of Feminism: Gender, Culture and Social Change*. London: Sage.

Merleau-Ponty, M. (1945; 2012) *The Phenomenology of Perception*, Trans. D. A. Landes, New York: Routledge.

Merrick (2007) 'Capone with Frank Oz About Death at a Funeral, What Went Wrong on Stepford, and (Of Course) Yoda!!' *Ain't It Cool* August 7.

Moers, E. (1978) 'Female Gothic' *Literary Women*, London: The Women's Press: 90-110.

Monahan, M. (2004) 'A Wife Less Ordinary', *The Telegraph* June 26.

Mori, M. (1970; 2012) 'The Uncanny Valley' trans K. F. MacDorman and N. Kageki. *IEEE Robotics and Automation Magazine*: 98-100.

Murphy, B.M. (2009) *The Suburban Gothic in American Popular Culture*, New York: Palgrave.

Murphy A. D. (1971) 'Tax Break to Ease Pix Crisis "Schreiber Plan" to Cut Charges,' *Variety* September 15, 3.

_____. (1972) 'Film Trade Sanity Asserts Itself: Inventory Down From Crazy Highs.' *Variety* April 12: 3; 20.

_____. (1976) '300 Indi Films pace Production: Invest $100-Mil Outside Majors' *Variety* June 9: 1.

Nadarajan, G. (2007) 'Islamic Automation: A Reading of Al Jazari's *The Book of Knowledge of Ingenious Mechanical Devices* (1206), Foundation for Science, Technology, and Civilisation.

Negra, D. (2009) *What a Girl Wants? Fantasizing the Reclamation of Self in Postfeminism*, New York: Routledge.

Nuss, L. (2004) 'New Stepford Wives Fuels Old Anti Career Views' womensenews.org, July 7.

Owsianik, J. and R. Dawson. Future of Sex Report. https://futureofsex.net/

Paul, W. (1977) 'Hollywood Harakiri' *Film Comment* 13.2: 62.

Projansky, S. (2001) *Watching Rape: Film and Television in Postfeminist Culture*, New York: New York University Press.

Pugliese, J. (2002) 'Race as Category Crisis: Whiteness and the Topical Assignation of Race', *Social Semiotics* 12.2: 149-68.

Punter, D. (2007) 'The Uncanny', pp. 129-36 in C. Spooner and E. McEvoy (eds) *The Routledge Companion to the Gothic*, Hoboken: Taylor & Francis.

_____ and G. Byron (2004) *The Gothic*, Chichester: Wiley-Blackwell.

Quart, A. (July-August 2004) 'Our Bodies, Our Selves: The Stepford Wives', *Film Comment*.

Radcliffe, A. (1794) *The Mysteries of Udolpho*, London: G.G. and J. Robinson, Paternoster-Row.

Riviere, J. (1929) 'Womanliness as a Masquerade,' *International Journal of Psycho-Analysis*: 303-313.

Robertson, J. (2010) 'Gendering Humanoid Robots: Robo-Sexism in Japan', *Body & Society* 16/2: 28.

Rosemary's Baby Review (1968), *Variety*, May 29: 6.

_____. (1968) *Boxoffice*, June 3: 4118.

Royle, N. (2003) *The Uncanny*, Manchester: Manchester University Press.

Russ, J. (1973) 'Somebody's Trying to Kill Me and I Think It's My Husband: The Modern Gothic,' *Journal of Popular Culture* 6.4: 666-691.

Ruston, S. (2005) *Shelley and Vitality*, London: Palgrave.

Sandler, S. (1992). 'Ira Levin: Oral History Memoir', American Jewish Committee Oral History Library.

Schickel, R. (1975) 'Women's Glib' *Time* 105.9: 2-3.

Schweishelm, K. (2012) 'Remaking *The Stepford Wives*, Remodelling Feminism', pp. 107-121 in K. Loock and C. Verevis (eds) *Film Remakes, Adaptions and Fan Productions: Remake/Remodel*, London: Palgrave.

Scott, A. O. (2004) 'Married to a Machine' *The New York Times*, June 11.

Seton, Anya. (1945) *Dragonwyck*, Great Britain: Hodder & Stoughton.

'Sex, Society, and the Female Dilemma: A Dialogue between Simone de Beauvoir and Betty Friedan' *Saturday Review*, 14th June, 1975: 14-20.

Shanley, M. (1989) *Feminism, Marriage, and the Law in Victorian England 1850-1895*, New Jersey: Limelight.

Shelley-Wollstonecraft, M. (1818) *Frankenstein: Or the Modern Prometheus*, Boston and Cambridge: Sever, Frances, & Co.

Sherry, E. (1948) *Sudden Fear*, New York: Dodo, Mead, & Company.

Shorter, E. and D. Healy. (2006) *Shock Therapy: A History of Electroconvulsive Treatment in Mental Illness*, New Jersey, Rutgers.

Showalter, E. A. (1982) *Literature of Their Own: British Women Novelists From Brontë to Lessing*. London: Verso.

_____. (1980) 'Victorian Women and Insanity' *Victorian Studies* 23.2: 157-81.

Sobchack, V. (1986) 'Child/Alien/Father: Patriarchal Crisis and Generic Exchange', *Camera Obscura* 5.3: 6-35.

_____. (2005) 'American Science Fiction Film' pp. 259-274, in S. Seed (ed.) *A Companion to Science Fiction*, New Jersey: Blackwell.

Smith, A. and D. Wallace, (2004) 'The Female Gothic: Then and Now', *Gothic Studies* 6.1: 1-7.

Soare, M. (2008) 'Return of the Female Gothic: The Career-Woman-in-Peril Thriller' pp. 88-119 in M. Brock (ed.) *Situating the Feminist Gaze and Spectatorship in Postwar Cinema*, Newcastle Upon Tyne: Cambridge Scholars Publishing.

Socarides C. W. (1974) 'The Demonified Mother: A Study of Voyeurism and Sexual Sadism,' *International Review of Psychoanalysis* 1: 187-195.

'Station Wagon and Movie Title Contests Used to Promote 'The Stepford Wives'' *Boxoffice* June 23, 1975: 34.

Stepford Wives, The, Review (1975) *The Independent Film Journal* 75.5 Feb 19: 6.

_____. Review (1975) *Variety* Feb 12: 28.

_____. Review (1975) *Boxoffice* Feb 17: 4758.

_____. Promotional Poster (1974) *Variety* November 6: 21.

_____. Promotional Poster (1974) *Variety* November 27: 15.

_____. Promotional Poster (1974) *Variety* December 18: 25.

'Stepford Wives Filming Begins in Westport, Conn' (1974) *Boxoffice* June 17: NE6.

'"Stepford'" Sequel Set' (1979) *Variety*, December 5: 54.

Stephens, E. (2015) '"Dead Eyes Open": The Role of Experiments in Galvanic Reanimation in Nineteenth-Century Popular Culture', *Leonardo* 48.3: 276-277.

Stevenson, R. L. (1886) *The Strange Case of Dr Jekyll and Mr Hyde*, Oxford: Oxford University Press.

Stoker, B. (1897; 2000) *Dracula*. London: Dover Publications.

Stratton, J. (1996) *The Desirable Body: Cultural Fetishism and the Erotics of Consumption*, Manchester: Manchester University Press.

Studlar, G. (1984) 'Macochism and the Perverse Pleasures of the Cinema', *Quarterly Review of Film Studies*: 267-282.

_____. (1985) 'Visual Pleasure and the Masochistic Aesthetic', *Journal of Film and Video*, 37.2: 5-26.

_____. (1990) 'Masochism, Masquerade, and the Erotic Metamorphosis of Marlene Dietrich,' pp.229-249, in J.Gaines and C. Herzog (eds) *Fabrications: Costume and the Female Body*, New York: Routledge.

Tasker, Y. and D. Negra (2007) *Interrogating Postfeminism: Gender Politics of Popular Culture*, Durham: Duke University Press.

Tay, S. (2003) 'Constructing a Feminist Cinematic Genealogy: The Gothic Woman's Film Beyond Psychoanalysis,' *Women: A Cultural Review* 14.3: 263-280.

Taylor, A. (2012) *Single Women in Popular Culture: The Limits of Postfeminism,* New York: Palgrave.

Taylor, S. (1938) 'The Suburban Neurosis' *The Lancet*: 759-62.

Thompson, B. (2002) 'Multiracial Feminism: Recasting the Chronology of Second Wave Feminism,' *Feminist Studies* 28.2 Second Wave Feminism in the United States: 336-60.

Trigell, J. (1991) *Introduction to Sliver*, Ira Levin, New York: Bantam Dell.

Turing, A. (1950) 'Computing Machinery and Intelligence', *Mind* 59/236: 433–60.

Van Driel, M. (2012) *With the Hand: A Cultural History of Masturbation*, Trans. Paul Vincent, London: Reaktion.

Vartanian, A. (1960) *LaMattrie's L'Homme Machine: A Study in the Origins of an Idea*, New Jersey: Princeton University Press.

Vizzini, B. E. (2008) 'Cold War Fears, Cold War Passions: Conservatives and Liberals Square Off in 1950s Science Fiction', *Quarterly Review of Film and Video* 26.1: 28-39.

Wajcman, J. (1991) *Feminism Confronts Technology*, Pennsylvania: Pennsylvania State University.

Ward, A. (1976) 'Cut To: William Goldman. The Screenwriter as Millionaire,' *American Film* Jan 1: 29-32.

Walpole, H. (1764; 1966) *The Castle of Otranto*, London: Dover Publications.

Weiser, Mark. (July 1993) 'Some Computer Science Issues in Ubiquitous Computing,' *Communications of the ACM* 36.7: 75-84.

Wells H. G. (1896) *The Island of Dr Moreau*, London: Harper Collins, 2017.

Whelehan, I. (2000) *Overloaded: Popular Culture and the Future of Feminism*, London: Palgrave.

_____. (2010) 'Rethinking Feminism: Or Why is Postfeminism So Boring?' *Nordic Journal of English Studies*: 155-172.

Williams, A. (2007) '*The Stepford Wives*: What's a Living Doll to Do in a Postfeminist World?' pp. 85-92, in B. Brabon and S. Genz (eds) *Postfeminist Gothic: Critical Interventions in Contemporary Culture*: London: Palgrave.

Wood, E. (1861; 2000) *East Lynne*. Edited by Andrew Maunder, Toronto: Broadview.

Woodcroft, B. (2015) *Pneumatica: The Pneumatics of Hero of Alexandria*, New York: Oia.

Wosk, J. (2015) *My Fair Ladies: Female Robots, Androids, and Other Artificial Eyes*, New Jersey: Rutgers University Press.

Wyndham, J. (1957) *The Midwich Cuckoos*, New York: Rosetta.

Endnotes

1. First published in serial form in the weekly art and literature review *La Vie Modern* (*The Modern Life*, 1885-1886).
2. Some other examples of creative works that explore the dark underbelly of the suburbs include the literature of Shirley Jackson and Joyce Carroll Oates, as well as the films *The Burbs* (Joe Dante, 1989), *The Stepfather* (Joseph Ruben, 1987), and *Happiness* (Todd Solondz, 1998).
3. The 2017 black comedy *Suburbicon* (directed by George Clooney and written by Joel and Ethan Coen) offers a poignant critique of Levittown. It also features footage from the 1957 documentary *Crisis in Levittown*, which underscores the suburbs as a hotbed for racism.
4. Shirley Jackson's short story 'The Beautiful Stranger' (1968) captures the essence of women's experiences in 1950s suburbs with powerful effect.
5. Other notable automatons to emerge in the 1700s are Japanese Zashiki Karakuri. Originally luxury entertainment items for feudal lords during the Edo period, they include the 'Chahakobi Ningyo' (tea serving doll) and the Yumihiki Doji (archer doll) (Boyle http://www.karakuri.info). Another well-known automation is an extravagant silver swan, created by John Joseph Merlin and James Cox in 1773. The swan, which is housed at The Bowes Museum (Teesdale, UK), twists its head to preen itself and catches a fish from the twisted glass stream on which it rests.
6. This said, innovations such as the Boston Dynamics robot 'Atlas' are both clearly machine and uncanny. Much of this has to do with the way Atlas moves. It is obviously a robot, but its human-like form and actions present a loss of affinity, as described by Mori (1970, p.99), that destabilises innate assumptions about the distinction between living species and machines in much the same way that Vaucanson's mechanical duck and other early automatons.
7. Ray Bradbury's short story 'Marionettes, Inc.' (1949) explores the technophobic possibility of robots that not only look lifelike, but consider themselves to be alive.
8. The pseudoscience of Phrenology – derived from the theories of Franz Joseph Gall (1758-1828), which involved measuring bumps on the skull to determine mental states was also influential to the logics of Social Darwinism.
9. Several scenes in *The Stepford Wives* are also shot at the Goodwives Shopping Centre, which actually exists in the town of Darien, Connecticut.
10. A&P (The Great Atlantic and Pacific Tea Company) was a US grocery store chain that operated until 2015.
11. It is telling of contemporary gender politics that *Charlie's Angels* continues to be remade for cinema: *Charlies Angels* (McG, 2000); *Charlie's Angels: Full Throttle* (McG, 2003) and *Charlie's Angels* (Elizabeth Banks, 2019).

12. In his book *Betty Friedan and the Making of the Feminine Mystique* (1998) Daniel Horowitz presents a revealing and detailed study of the life of Friedan (formerly Bettye Goldstein) including the hidden connections between her union activity of the 1940s and early 1950s and the feminism she articulated in the 1960s. The book is an interesting read for those interested in discovering more about Friedan.
13. See *Vogue* (1975) ''Danger Ahead'' Valium: The Pill You Love Can Turn on You': pp.152-3.
14. From The Rolling Stones' 1966 song 'Mother's Little Helper': 'Mother needs something today to calm her down/And though she's not really ill/There's a little yellow pill/She goes running for the shelter of a mother's little helper/And it helps her on her way, gets her through her busy day'.
15. Other thrillers that follow in the tracks of *Fatal Attraction* include *Basic Instinct* (Paul Verhoeven, 1992), *The Temp* (Tom Holland, 1993), *Disclosure* (Barry Levinson, 1994), and *The Last Seduction* (John Dahl, 1994). All of these films problematize successful career women, depicting them as unhinged, conniving, and murderous.
16. According to Oz, this was not the originally intended opening. He planned for the film to begin with a wide angle long shot of a Manhattan street filled with thousands of women wearing black, but it did not work out the way he intended, so it was changed to the vintage montage described.
17. Bonnie Dow also discusses postfeminist themes of choice in *The Stepford Wives* remake (See Dow, 2006, pp.113-31).
18. Descartes is reported to have secretly brought a life sized replica of his deceased daughter Francine on a sea voyage to Sweden in the 1600s as company. Allegedly, the doll, made of leather and metal, was so lifelike that when discovered by the ship's crew, it triggered such profound revulsion that they threw it overboard (Ferguson, 2010, p.17).
19. From John Sigden's translation of Schwaeblé's *Les Détraqués de Paris* pp.247-53 (in Levy, 2009, p.179): 'Every one of them takes at least three months of my work! There's the inner framework which is carefully articulated, there's the hair on the head, the body hair, the teeth, the nails! There's the skin, which has to be given a certain tint, certain contours, a particular pattern of veins. There are the eyes, which need to be given some expression, there's the tongue, and I don't know what else. You won't find a waxwork or a statue, not even the ones created by the great masters that can be compared to my products. The only thing these haven't got is the power of speech!' (From a discussion with 'Dr. P' regarding his craft).
20. See http://realbotix.com
21. As of this writing, sex doll brothels are emerging phenomena. Japan has had them for some time, mainly located in Tokyo, but they are expanding. Sex doll brothels can be found in London, Paris, Barcelona, Moscow, Helsinki, Aarhus, Vienna, Turin, Toronto, and Vancouver. This has gained considerable attention from mainstream media, where stories generally

focus on the ethics of offering such services. Central concerns are that sex doll brothels promote the objectification of women; that they normalise more extreme sex practices; and that human sex workers will become redundant (see Kerr, 2018 and Dickson, 2018).

22. See FutureofSex.net
23. See Hanson Robotics https://www.hansonrobotics.com/bina48-9/
24. Further technologies anticipated to transfigure sexual practices and experiences such as state-of-the-art immersive entertainment that combines virtual reality with haptic sex devices, 360-degree perspectives and binaural sound, are expected to become increasingly common, as is the projection of 3D holographic imagery into people's immediate spaces. One example of the way holographs are starting to be used is Gatebox Inc.'s Azuma Hikari. Hikari is a figurine sized digital projection of a *bishōjo* (cute girl) anime character housed in a high-tech glass capsule designed to sit on a nightstand. Gatebox promotes Hikari as a 'bride' and perfect partner who will wake you in the morning, chat with you throughout the day, while you are out, via text message, and listen to you as you reflect back over the day's events in the evening. The Future of Sex Report predicts that holographs will also be used as digital overlays, transforming the appearance of a person (or robot) to make them look like a celebrity of instance. This concept is played out in *Blade Runner 2049* (Denis Villeneuve, 2017), where Joi (Ana de Armas), the holographic girlfriend of K (Ryan Gosling), superimposes herself over a sex worker for him. Spike Jonze's *Her* (2013) also focuses on similar technologies. Other augmented innovations include neural headsets that will enable mind melding and thought sharing; tissue engineering, implants, chips, and surgical techniques designed to customize the body and heighten its erotic responses; and neural implants and sensors made to stimulate the pleasure centers of the brain (FutureofSex.net).
25. For example, the online Campaign Against Sex Robots (https://campaignagainstsexrobots.org/).
26. http://oxygen.csail.mit.edu/Overview.html
27. The US government's investigation into U.F.O activity initiated in the 1950s was called 'Project Blue Book.'
28. While this book has focused on examples involving artificial women, the rape-revenge theme extends other narratives too. One recent examples is Leigh Whannell's 2020 version of *The Invisible Man*.

www.ingramcontent.com/pod-product-compliance
Lightning Source LLC
Chambersburg PA
CBHW071412300426
44114CB00016B/2277